How Religi[ ] are Engaging Young Adults in America

Monte Sahlin and David Roozen, Editors

2015

Faith Communities Today
Hartford, Connecticut

Faith Communities Today (FACT)
the research publications of the
Cooperative Congregational Studies Partnership

Table of Contents

Introduction

The consensus of current research finds a growing percentage of young adults in America are not connected with any religion, although many express an interest in spirituality. This reality is, not surprisingly, causing great concern among the leaders of most faith traditions. What to do about it, unfortunately, has remained elusive; thus the research presented in this volume.

The Cooperative Congregational Studies Partnership (CCSP) includes research professionals from almost all religions in the United States. The research partnership has worked together since the late 1990s in the largest, continuing study of local congregations, including among other things, trend-tracking national surveys of American congregations every five years (http://faithcommunitiestoday.org/). Most recently, the cooperative research effort has focused on the religious participation of young adults: What is the involvement of young adults in local congregations with the full spectrum of faith traditions in the United States? And, more importantly, how are faith communities with significant proportions of young adults distinctive in their ability to engage young adults? This book brings together that research.

For the purposes of the research, a congregation is considered to have significant young adult participation if 21 percent or more of its active participants were 18 to 34 years of age. Across all faiths, a total of only 16 percent of all congregations meet this criterion.

After reviewing the basic data from a large survey of over 10,000 American congregations, the research partners were driven to seek a more detailed and nuanced rendering of what congregations that are successfully engaging young adults look like. In response, CCSP decided to collect a set of case studies that describe the patterns and practices of congregations where a significant, exceptional number of young adults are involved. Those cases are the core of this volume, supplemented by the survey data and a summary of other research on the topic for broader perspective, as well as a summary of findings from the set of cases.

The case studies look at ten congregations across the spectrum of religions in America:

ChristWay Community Church, in Ooltewah, Tennessee, is a fast-growing church in suburban Chattanooga with Southern Baptist roots, a "Starbucks-like" feel, and about 800 regular attendees. A substantial number of young adults are integrated into the congregation, although it also has events and small groups specifically for people age 18 to 25.

Herriman Young Single Adult Ward is a suburban Salt Lake City-area congregation of the Church of Jesus Christ of Latter-Day Saints (LDS) with some 300 young adults led by a dynamic husband-and-wife team. Only officially one-year-old at the time of the research, the congregation was formed when the LDS ("Mormon" church) reorganized its young adults-only congregations. Some of its activities are gender-segregated, and young adults involved move on to other congregations when they marry or turn 31. The congregation stresses testimony and practical advice for dealing with issues such as addiction to pornography and being single and unhappy.

The Houston Baha'i' Center is a "mid-town" congregation established in 1942 by a religious faith that began in Iran. One in six of its attendees are between 18 and 30. Nearly one in 10 members of the congregation's board are young adults, and members of that age are heavily involved in teaching and mentoring the youth of the congregation.

Kirkwood United Church of Christ is a seven-year-old mainline Protestant congregation located in an Atlanta inner suburb. Founded by a dynamic couple, this congregation has been strongly involved in its neighborhood. About one in five of its 150 members is currently between 18 and 30 and students from Atlanta seminaries—many of them also young adults—have been leaders in the congregation.

Life Center Four Square Church, in suburban Spokane, Washington, is an Evangelical mega church; an 80-year-old Pentecostal congregation whose current pastor started in 1978. Life Center moved to its current location in 2005 with about 8,000 people affiliated with it. The congregation's third Sunday worship service includes a large contingent of young adults and events of its ministry for young people age 18 to 25 draw about 150. The congregation has also started five other congregations and intentional residential communities for college students.

New Life Covenant Church is a predominantly African American, 10-year-old congregation located near downtown Chicago. It has a dynamic founding pastor and four different young adult ministries. About 30 percent of its members are youths or young adults.

Saint Mary Orthodox Church in Cambridge, Massachusetts, has benefited from some of its pastors serving as chaplains for neighboring colleges and universities and at popular Orthodox camps. Founded in 1928 as an Arabic-speaking congregation of Syrian Americans, it has repositioned itself to serve Orthodox Christians of varying ethnicities and survived a financial scare in the 1990s. About a quarter of the 150 worshipers in a typical service are young adults.

Temple Micah is a Jewish Synagogue with some 500 member households. Its Next Dor DC ministry and one monthly service are targeted for young adults, who make up one in five of the worshipers. Events such as "Drink and Drash" also attract 20 or 30 young adults. The congregation, founded in 1963, has partnered with a cross-denominational Jewish organization and called a second Rabbi to reach out to people in their 20s and 30s.

The Well is an interdenominational ministry of Evangel Church, an Assemblies of God congregation located in suburban northeastern New Jersey near New York City. A 30-something couple has led this cross-denominational ministry since it was established in 2007. Weekly Well worship services feature about 40 to 60 people, while the larger Evangel Church includes about 1,700 in its various services.

Old Saint Patrick's Roman Catholic Church in downtown Chicago has some 3,500 registered households. Although the congregation was founded in 1846, it has connected with a totally new group of worshipers since the mid-1980s. Its Sunday evening worship service and events such as "Theology on Tap" and the "World's Largest Block Party" disproportionately attract young adults. Training for people new to the Catholic faith and for those preparing to marry also connects the church with many young adults.

Most of these congregations are not famous for their young adult ministry. Most do not consider themselves remarkable. On the whole, they are typical of local congregations in which a real effort is being made to connect with young adults and make them part of the religious life of the faith community. They sketch a picture of what the topic of young adult ministry looks like at the grass roots in America today.

A number of the authors of these case studies are young adults, while others have been involved in young adult ministry. Each was involved in personal observation of the congregation about which they wrote.

It is hoped that careful reading and rigorous reflection on these case studies will lead to not only a deeper understanding of how some congregations are effectively engaging young adults, but also the identification of best practices to reach this distinctive demographic segment. It is also hoped that the comparative analysis across congregations in widely different faith traditions will not only help to identify common strategies for engaging young adults, but also help particular faith groups more fully appreciate their distinct gifts and challenges. The final chapter highlights some key, practical elements that emerge from the case studies.

Monte Sahlin
March 2015

Chapter 1
A Profile of Congregations with Significant Young Adult Participation

By Monte Sahlin and David Roozen

The emerging consensus of research shows a growing percentage of young adults are not connected with any religion, although many of these express an interest in spirituality. (See Literature Review.) This reality, along with the general American demographic shift toward an older population, rightfully raises concern about young adult participation in religious communities. What is the involvement of young adults in local congregations of all faiths across the United States?

The most recent Faith Communities Today national survey of American congregations (FACT 2010) offers significant insight related to this topic. The national FACT survey is an amalgam of 26 individual surveys of congregations, 24 conducted by collaborating organizations representing 32 of the country's largest religious traditions and denominations. These were supplemented by two random samples of congregations not a part of collaborating organizations. The final dataset includes a just over 11,000 congregations. The common core questionnaire used in these surveys replicates over 150 items from the 2000, 2005 and 2008 surveys, and includes a special section on the 2008 recession. FACT is the largest ongoing research project in America focused on local religious bodies.

For purposes of this report a congregation is considered to have significant young adult participation if 21 percent or more of its participants were 18 to 34 years of age. Across all faiths, a total of only 15.8 percent of all congregations were in this category. Clearly, the congregations highlighted in this paper, those with significant young adult participation, are not typical of American religious congregations.

The percentage of congregations with significant young adult participation varied considerably among religious traditions and denominations. The first graph displays the percentage in each of 25 faith groups, of which 11 are at or above the overall average and 14 are below the average. The percentage ranges from 2.3 percent at the low end to 25.6 percent on the high end. Given this information, it would not be surprising if there is greater concern about young adult participation in some faith groups than in others.

Certain demographic factors relate significantly to young adult participation. A total of 22.5 percent of congregations where most of the members are from ethnic minority groups reported a significant number of young adult participants, while only 12.5 percent of congregations with a white majority reported the same. There is a similar contrast among congregations located in metropolitan areas and those outside the metropolitan areas. (See Graph 3.) Nearly a quarter of the congregations located in newer suburbs had a significant level of young adult participation, as did one in five of the congregations located in cities and older suburbs. Only 12 percent of the congregations located in small towns and rural regions outside the metropolitan areas reported the same level of young adult participation.

There was less variance among the major regions of the United States. (See Graph 2.) The highest proportion of congregations with significant young adult participation was in the west. The South and Midwest were near the national average, while a lower percentage of congregations in the northeast gave the same report.

How young adult participation may correlate with the size of congregation is less clear in these data, although a mid-size range may be optimal to engage young adults. (See Graph 5.) Congregations with a typical weekend attendance of 301 to 350 were more likely to report a significant percentage of young adult participation than were those congregations with either less or greater attendance. Congregations with higher young adult participation than the national average ranged from 151 to 400 in attendance or had a typical attendance of more than 500 people. Small congregations with an attendance of 150 or less were least likely to report a significant level of young adults.

The correlation between staffing and young adult participation is much clearer. (See Graph 6.) The conventional pattern of staffing for American congregations is to have one, full-time clergy person and congregations with this staffing were least likely to have a significant level of young adult participation. Congregations with no full-time clergy were more likely to have a significant percentage of young adults, although less than average. A significantly higher percentage of congregations with young adults reported having two or more full-time clergy.

Congregations with rapid growth (more than ten percent over the previous decade) were significantly more likely to report young adult participation. (See Graph 7.) Perhaps surprisingly, those with rapid decline (a loss of more than ten percent in the previous decade) were the next most likely to have a significant level of young adults, although below the overall average. Congregations with modest levels of growth or decline (less than ten percent in the previous decade) were least likely to have a significant number of young adults. Does this suggest that there is something about relatively stable-state congregations that is least attractive to young adults?

The use of new technology is clearly correlated with young adult participation. Those congregations that reported major usage of technology were more than twice as likely to have a significant percentage of young adults than those who reported only marginal use. Nearly one in four congregations (24 percent) were in the first category and only ten percent were in the second group. A little less than an average percentage of congregations reporting modest use of technology (14 percent) had significant numbers of young adults.

There is also a clear correlation between young adult participation and offering a menu of programs and activities. (See Graph 9.) The more programs reported by a congregation the more likely it was that the congregation was among those reporting a significant number of young adults. Congregations reporting many programs were nearly twice as likely to have significant young adult participation as those reporting few or some programs.

A similar correlation was found with the number of men in the congregation. Those congregations with relatively few women (a quarter of less) were twice as likely to have a significant share of young adults. In other words, the more men there were in a congregation the more likely it was to attract young adults. (See Graph 10.)

One of the strongest correlations among the FACT 2010 data is the relationship between how recently a congregation was begun and the level of young adult participation. (See Graph 11.) New congregations organized in the previous decade were more than three times as likely as those organized before 1976 to have a significant number of young adults. Even those congregations founded from 1976 through 1999 were more than twice as likely to have a significant number of young adults than the older congregations. Is it clear that religious organizations need to be planting new congregations for new generations?

Much has been written about attracting young adults by changing worship styles and music, yet the FACT 2010 surveys do not provide as strong a correlation as might be expected. Congregations that reported their worship style had "changed a lot" in the previous five years were more likely to have significant young adult participation, but congregations that reported no change were also somewhat more likely to have a significant number of young adults and the percentage of young adults for those congregations that reported "little" or "some" change in worship style reported only an average level of young adult participation. (See Graph 12.) At least it appears that this concept must be more nuanced than an across-the-board principle for engaging young adults in all faiths and contexts.

The relationship between new worship styles and young adult participation is clearer in the data about the use of the electric guitar or bass and projectors. (See Graph 13.) Congregations that reported using these items in their worship "often" or "always" were about twice as likely as those who never used them to have significant numbers of young adults participating. Using the electric guitar or bass "sometimes" was least likely to attract young adults. Further evidence is found in a combined measure of how often an electric guitar or bass and a drum are used. Those congregations that reported using these musical instruments "always" or "often" were twice as likely to have a significant number of young adults as were congregations that reported using them less often if at all. Is this strong evidence that a contemporary worship style is an important part of engaging young adults, at least in many faith communities?

Congregations that emphasize basic spiritual practices are generally more likely to attract young adults. (See Graph 15.) In the FACT 2010 surveys, congregations that indicated they place "quite a bit" or "a lot" of emphasis on teaching spiritual practices were twice as likely to have a significant number of young adult participants as those who gave the topic only "some" or "little" emphasis. The difference between those congregations that reported "no emphasis" and "a lot" was five times greater. It appears that congregations that teach spiritual practices are attractive to young adults.

There was also a strong correlation between the spiritual vitality of a congregation and engagement with young adults. Congregations that reported high spiritual vitality were three times as likely to have a significant number of young adults. Only seven percent of the congregations reporting low spiritual vitality also reported a significant number of young adult participants, while 21 percent of those reporting high spiritual vitality also reported significant young adult participation. Among congregations reporting moderate spiritual vitality, 14.8 percent also reported significant young adult participation.

If a congregation initiates serious efforts to engage young adults using means appropriate to its faith tradition and context, will that result in attracting a larger proportion of young adults among its regular participants? The FACT 2010 surveys asked congregations how much emphasis they placed on young adult activities or programs. Overall, nearly a third (31 percent) reported that they had no such activities, about another third (38 per cent) reported "some emphasis" on young adult activities, one in four (24 percent) report "a lot of emphasis" on young adult activities and 7.5 percent said it was "a specialty of the congregation."

Congregations that reported the greatest emphasis on young adult ministry, were twice as likely to also report engaging a significant number of young adults. Congregations that reported "a lot of emphasis" on young adult activities and programs were also more likely to engage a significant number of young adults, while those that reported only "some emphasis" were less likely to attract young adults. Those congregations that reported no young adult activities were less than half as likely to have a significant number of young adult participants.

David Roozen, Ph.D., is director of the Hartford Institute for Religion Research and a faculty member at Harford Seminary, as well as chairman of the Cooperative Congregational Studies Partnership (CCSP), author of several books and a papers on religion in America. Monte Sahlin serves as executive secretary of CCSP. Before retiring, he taught in the Doctor of Ministry program at Andrews University, in urban studies at Eastern University and served as a senior research officer for the Seventh-day Adventist Church.

Graph 1

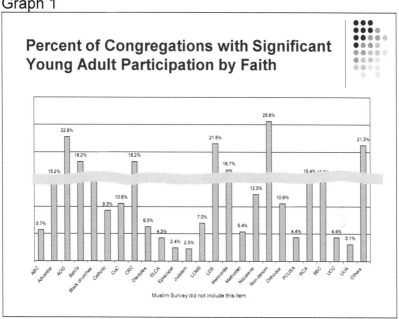

Percent of Congregations with Significant Young Adult Participation by Faith

Muslim Survey did not include this item.

Graph 2

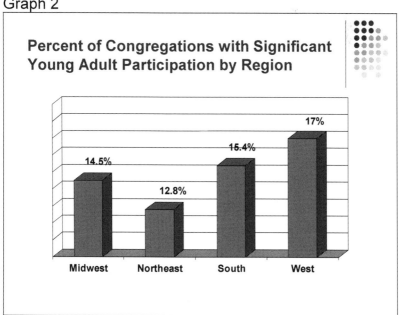

Percent of Congregations with Significant Young Adult Participation by Region

Graph 3

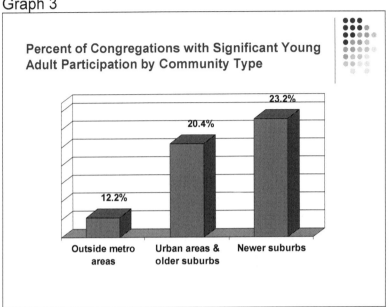

Percent of Congregations with Significant Young Adult Participation by Community Type

- 23.2% — Newer suburbs
- 20.4% — Urban areas & older suburbs
- 12.2% — Outside metro areas

Graph 4

Percent of Congregations with Significant Young Adult Participation by Ethnicity

- There is a strong correlation between ethnic diversity and engagement with young adults.

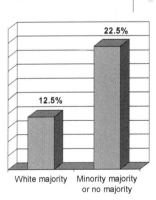

- 22.5% — Minority majority or no majority
- 12.5% — White majority

Graph 5

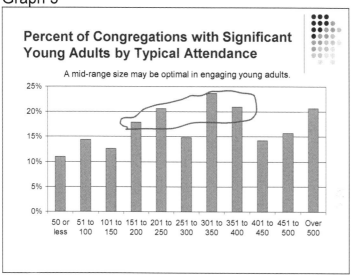

Percent of Congregations with Significant Young Adults by Typical Attendance

A mid-range size may be optimal in engaging young adults.

Graph 6

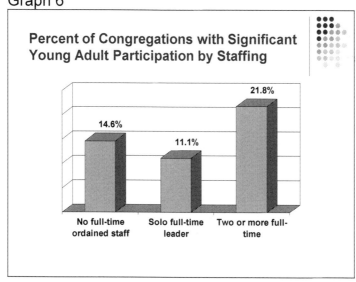

Percent of Congregations with Significant Young Adult Participation by Staffing

Graph 7

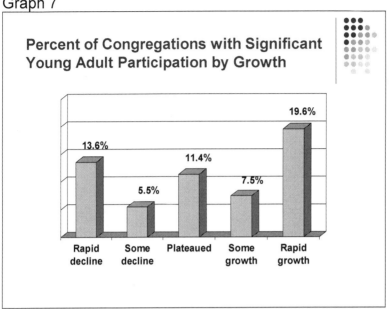

Percent of Congregations with Significant Young Adult Participation by Growth

13.6% Rapid decline
5.5% Some decline
11.4% Plateaued
7.5% Some growth
19.6% Rapid growth

Graph 8

Percent of Congregations with Significant Young Adult Participation by Technology

- There is a clear correlation between use of technology by congregations and engagement with young adults.

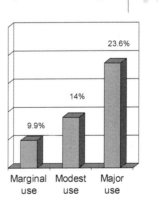

9.9% Marginal use
14% Modest use
23.6% Major use

Graph 9

Percent of Congregations with Significant Young Adult Participation by Programs

- There is a clear correlation between the number of programs a congregations provides and engagement with young adults.

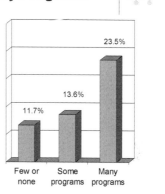

Graph 10

Percent of Congregations with Significant Young Adult Participation by Gender

- There is a negative correlation with the proportion of women in a congregation and its engagement with young adults. Stated as a positive, the more men there are in a congregation the more likely it is to engage young adults.

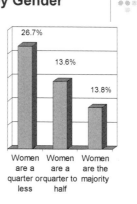

Graph 11

Percent of Congregations with Significant Young Adult Participation by Year Begun

- There is a correlation between more recently organized congregations and engagement with young adults.

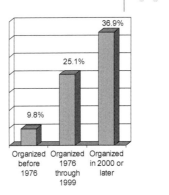

Graph 12

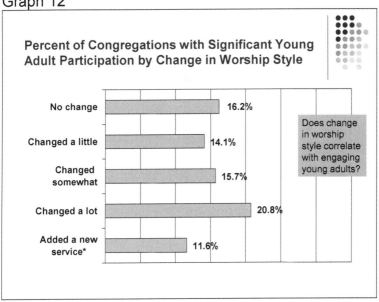

Percent of Congregations with Significant Young Adult Participation by Change in Worship Style

No change	16.2%
Changed a little	14.1%
Changed somewhat	15.7%
Changed a lot	20.8%
Added a new service*	11.6%

Does change in worship style correlate with engaging young adults?

Graph 13

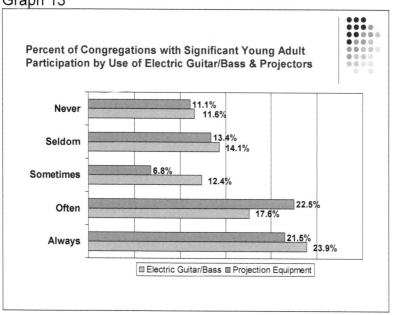

Percent of Congregations with Significant Young Adult Participation by Use of Electric Guitar/Bass & Projectors

Never — 11.1% / 11.6%
Seldom — 13.4% / 14.1%
Sometimes — 6.8% / 12.4%
Often — 22.5% / 17.6%
Always — 21.5% / 23.9%

Electric Guitar/Bass ▨ Projection Equipment

Graph 14

Percent of Congregations with Significant Young Adult Participation by Contemporary Worship

- There is a strong correlation between contemporary worship (measured by how often guitars and drums are used) and engagement with young adults.

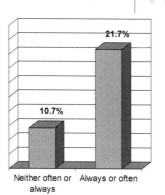

10.7%   21.7%

Neither often or always   Always or often

Graph 15

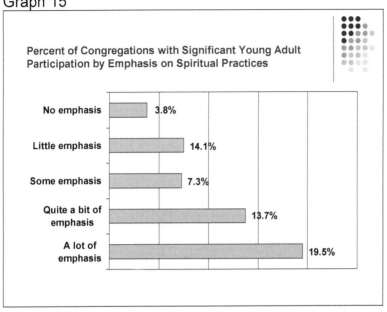

Percent of Congregations with Significant Young Adult Participation by Emphasis on Spiritual Practices

No emphasis	3.8%
Little emphasis	14.1%
Some emphasis	7.3%
Quite a bit of emphasis	13.7%
A lot of emphasis	19.5%

Graph 16

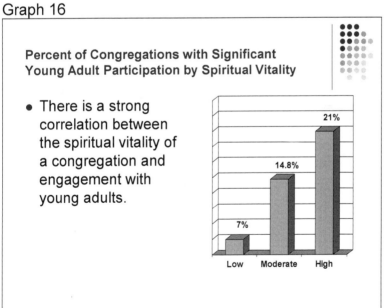

Percent of Congregations with Significant Young Adult Participation by Spiritual Vitality

- There is a strong correlation between the spiritual vitality of a congregation and engagement with young adults.

7% (Low) 14.8% (Moderate) 21% (High)

Chapter 2
A Review of Previous Research

By LiErin Probasco

For the majority of 18 to 29 year olds, organized religion could be described as "mostly harmless." Relatively few young adults are hostile toward religion, but one-third are religiously unaffiliated (Lugo 2012), and over half describe church as irrelevant (Smith 2009). "Mostly harmless" are the words Douglas Adams' novel *The Hitchhiker's Guide to the Galaxy* used to describe the planet Earth shortly before it was slated for demolition to make way for an intergalactic highway.

Despite these statistics, the demise of congregational life as the U.S. has known it is in no way imminent. About one-third of US churchgoers attend a congregation where 35 percent or more of regularly participating adults are under 35 (Wuthnow 2007). What is it about these congregations that draws young adults? What might other congregations do to become relevant to the spiritually open but religiously indifferent?

To answer these questions, I will review recent studies of "vital congregations" that have strong participation of younger adults (Wuthnow 2007). I begin by describing the place of religion in the changing life worlds of those in their late teens to mid-thirties. Next, I briefly describe the current landscape of young adult religious participation in the United States. After providing these contexts, I will turn to ethnographic case studies of successful congregations.

Historian Diane Winston calls the "gold standard for organized religion" an encounter participants experience as authentic, accessible, and animating (2007, p 266). I argue that four practices are key to crafting such an encounter for young adults: articulating a core *identity*; *inclusion* of people with diverse religious and social backgrounds; worship and mentors that *inspire* participants to strive to be better people; and the flexibility and drive to *innovate*. Across religious traditions, geographic settings, and theological commitments, vital congregations embody these four themes in ways that respond to the uncertainty and promise that mark young adult lives.

Religion and the Life Worlds of Younger Adults

The paths people take from adolescence to adulthood are longer and more varied than ever before. In the United States, young adults marry and have children at later ages, pursue higher education at greater rates, and change jobs and residences frequently. They have unprecedented access to information about cultures and traditions that are not their own. Tolerance, diversity, and pluralism are values instilled by socializing institutions (such as families, schools, churches, and the media). The edited volume *On the Frontier of Adulthood* (Settersten, Furstenberg, and Rumbaut 2005) is a thorough academic introduction to these trends.

These changing life worlds shape young adults' religious beliefs and practices; in turn, religion can shape the ways young adults navigate their social landscapes. Below, I list several helpful concepts researchers have proposed for understanding how young adults' religious participation and changing life worlds influence one another.

Religion Among the Millennials is a 2010 report from the Pew Research Center. It documents the religious beliefs and practices of the "Millennial" generation (born roughly between 1981 and 1992). It also compares the practices of these 18-29-year-olds [at the time of this writing] to earlier generations' behaviors. Millennials are significantly less likely to affiliate with a congregation or attend worship services than previous generations did at ages 18-29. On the other hand, Millennials report many traditional beliefs (such as belief in heaven) and practices (such as frequent prayer). There is also great diversity within the generation.

Researchers compare birth cohorts based on the belief that shared experiences during formative years make people within a birth cohort ("Baby Boomers" or "Millennials") similar to one another and different from those born before or after. A generational approach can be useful for highlighting differences across cohorts, but it can sometimes mask important differences in life experiences within birth cohorts. Moreover, studies often investigate a generation *during* its younger adult years, making it difficult to distinguish between the durable characteristics that will follow that generation over time, and effects of lifecycle stages. Researchers or church leaders hoping to apply generational theories must pay careful attention to such distinctions.

Emerging Adulthood is a term introduced by psychologist Jeffrey Arnett. He argues that sweeping social changes have ushered in a new developmental stage between adolescence and adulthood. This period of "emerging adulthood" is characterized by intense self-focus and identity exploration; instability; a feeling of being "in between"; and hope in the possibilities the future holds (Arnett 2004).

In her book *Big Questions, Worthy Dreams*, Sharon Daloz Parks frames the primary developmental task of young adulthood as learning how to ask big enough questions and to cultivate dreams that are not simply ambitious but worthwhile. She outlines a praxis of mentoring aimed to draw out these worthy dreams and suggests congregations may be one place where such mentoring relationships can thrive. Her theory of young adult faith development suggests the extreme cultural relativism many young adults express is a functional but typically temporary phase in the process of becoming a self-actualized adult.

Moralistic Therapeutic Deism describes the vast majority of 18-23-year-olds' religious beliefs, regardless of religious tradition. According to sociologist Christian Smith, the basic tenets of moralistic therapeutic deism include belief that: (1) God created and watches over the world. (2) God wants people to be good, nice, and fair to one another. (3) The main goal in life is to be happy. (4) God does not need to be involved in one's life other than to resolve problems. (5) Good people go to heaven when they die (Smith and Denton 2005).

Smith and colleagues developed the concept of moralistic therapeutic deism to describe the religious beliefs of teens aged 13-17. In a second wave of research, they found these same teens continued to espouse moralistic therapeutic deism at ages 18-23. In fact, contrary to popular imagination, Smith and colleagues found young adult religiosity is strongly continuous with youth experiences. Young adults' relationships with parents and other engaged adults as teens are important predictors of their religious beliefs and practices as emerging adults (Smith 2009).

This study also finds the majority of 18-23-year-olds see congregations as places that teach right from wrong. Smith argues that most young adults feel confident they know right from wrong; they also tend to believe each individual has his or her own standards of right and wrong. This relativism explains, at least in part, why some appreciate what churches have to offer but most feel little need to explore questions of meaning or purpose in the context of a faith community. Smith does not clarify whether he believes this relativism is tied to a lifecycle stage (as Daloz-Parks argues) or a durable characteristic of the current generation of young adults.

Spiritual Tinkering describes a way of making meaning out of diverse ideas, symbols, and practices. Sociologist Robert Wuthnow's *After the Baby Boomers* (2007) suggests *tinkering* is a helpful metaphor for describing the religious orientations of younger adults, which he broadly defines as 18-44-year-olds. Tinkerers improvise with the resources at hand, making a life out of diverse, sometimes inconsistent, elements: orthodox and heterodox beliefs, Western and Eastern practices, Christian exceptionalism and religious tolerance. Tinkering is not a stage of faith formation but rather a pervasive orientation toward meaning-making which is particularly well adapted to a mobile, unpredictable, and diverse society. People of all ages tinker; however, Wuthnow argues that younger adults are especially adept tinkerers. They are experiencing an unstable stage of the lifecycle, and they have grown up in an era of rapidly expanding access to information and significant uncertainty about economic and social futures.

Faith Typologies capture the diversity of young adult religiosity by sorting young adults into categories. Christian Smith's *Souls in Transition* identifies six types of young adult orientations to religion: the committed traditionalists (15 percent), selective adherents (30 percent) the spiritually open (15 percent), the religiously indifferent (25 percent), the religiously disconnected (5 percent), and the irreligious (10 percent). Other typologies exist within particular faith traditions. Flory and Miller (2008) describe four kinds of religiously active Christian young adults: innovators, appropriators, resisters, and reclaimers. Hayes (2007) lists seven ways Catholic young engage religion. Ukeles, Miller, and Beck (2006) see four major "life status" categories of Jewish young adults: the Orthodox, those married with children, those unmarried or married without children, and those who are married to someone who is not also Jewish.

The existence of so many ways to categorize young adult faith points to the incredible diversity within the current generation of young adults. However, to date, few typologies have been adopted or tested in subsequent research. Until they are, their reliability and validity as measures of meaningful intra-generational difference are uncertain.

Young Adult Religious Participation: An Overview

Despite an increase in non-affiliation, private religious beliefs and practices have generally high salience for younger adults. The 2004 College Students' Beliefs and Values (CSBV) Survey found 80 percent of incoming first year students report an interest in spirituality, and 47 percent say it is "very important" or "essential" to seek out opportunities to grow spiritually (Astin, Astin, and Lindholm 2005). When NSYR researchers asked 18-23-year-olds if they had become more religious, less religious, or stayed about the same over the past two years, most reported staying the same (59 percent) or becoming *more* religious (24 percent) (Smith 2009). Since at least the 1970s, young adults' private forms of religiosity – such as daily prayer, belief in life after death, and belief in Biblical inerrancy – have largely held at steady rates. Wuthnow and Smith both caution against drawing too sharp a distinction between "private" spirituality and "public" religiosity, however. Young adults themselves may not delineate such practices as strongly as researchers do. Wuthnow finds a majority of 21-45-year-olds (55 percent) describe themselves as *both* spiritual and religious, while Smith argues that a majority of 18-23-year-olds may be open to spirituality but are simply not all that interested in *either* religion or spirituality as a regular practice.

When it comes to public or collective religious participation, church attendance is the most common measure of engagement. Smith reports 20 percent of 18-23-year-olds attend frequently (weekly or more), while 35 percent never attend. Attendance rates vary across religious groups. Higher-than-average rates of frequent attendance can be found among Mormon, Conservative Protestant, and Black Protestant young adults, while Roman Catholic, Mainline Protestant, Jewish, and non-affiliated young adults all report lower than average rates of frequent attendance (Smith 2009).

Since the mid-1970s, there has been a modest decline in rates of regular (weekly or more) church attendance among young adults, from 19 percent to 15 percent of 18-25-year-olds, and from 31 percent to 25 percent of 21-45-year-olds (Smith 2009; Wuthnow 2007). Not all groups report declining attendance, however; among 18-25-year-olds, evangelical and black Protestants have seen slightly *increasing* rates of regular attendance, while Catholics and mainline Protestants' attendance rates have dropped (Smith 2009).

Wuthnow finds the two strongest predictors of church attendance among 21-45-year-olds are marital status and number of children; therefore, declining attendance rates (and differences in decline across denominations) can "almost entirely" be explained by changes in the timing of marriage and timing and number of children. Smith and Snell corroborate that other demographic considerations, such as gender, educational attainment, and income, have little effect on the trajectory of declining attendance rates. These results diverge from earlier research that argued postsecondary education has a "liberalizing" effect on students' orthodox religious beliefs. Mayrl and Uecker's (2011) detailed analysis of NSYR data address this long-standing debate; they, too, find no evidence for a liberalizing effect of education on contemporary young adults.

That religious attendance is a matter of demographics rather than denominational differences is mixed news for congregations. They have little hope of boosting attendance by encouraging early marriage and childbearing. On the other hand, young adult attendance is not driven by distaste for denominational identities, ideological schism, or active distrust of institutions. Rather, Wuthnow suggests, innovative congregations from any tradition could offer social and institutional support that society has largely failed to provide single and childless younger adults.

Characteristics of "Vital Congregations"

More than three-quarters of young adults (18-44) already attend church at least occasionally. What kinds of churches do they attend? The National Congregations Survey estimates one-third of American churchgoers attend a congregation where 35 percent or more adults are 35 or younger (Wuthnow 2007). Compared to others, these "youthful" congregations are more likely to be urban, ethnically diverse, founded more recently, and have more children in attendance. They are on average larger, with a higher proportion of new worshippers, suggesting they may be growing more rapidly than older congregations. Youthful congregations are also more likely to use overhead projectors during worship and to supplement piano and organ music with drums and electric guitars.

Hackett (2010) finds similar results using different data (the US Congregational Life Survey) and a narrower definition of young adults. He finds congregations with at least 10 percent 18-29-year-olds are larger, more racially diverse, and have proportionally more men than congregations with fewer young adults. He also finds striking differences across Christian traditions; while 59 percent of evangelical and 31 percent of Catholic congregations meet the 10 percent threshold, only 10 percent of mainline Protestant churches do.

Wuthnow argues that differences between youthful and older congregations are largely a matter of proximity, not preference. Many young adults live in urban areas, and urban churches are more likely to be racially diverse. However, young adults are present in congregations of all sizes; fewer than one in five 21-45-year-olds attend a church with more than 1,000 members, and about one in five attends a church with less than 100. Wuthnow finds no evidence to suggest they prefer larger congregations (preference for diversity is another matter, which I discuss below). To understand what kinds of congregations appeal to younger adults, I turn from quantitative to qualitative research.

Findings from Case Studies

Case study research situates congregational practices within particular social locations, theological commitments, and cultural contexts. In examining particularity, researchers discern how congregations develop principles and practices that situate young adults' religious yearnings and doubts within the congregation's mission and identity.
Two recent research projects most inform this overview of qualitative research. The Changing Spirituality of Emerging Adults (or Changing SEA) project (http://www.changingsea.org/) includes eight profiles of best

practices in Christian congregations with a strong young adult presence. The profiles include two evangelical, three Catholic, and three mainline/progressive congregations, all in urban settings. Six are large with a sizeable minority of young adults; two are small, predominantly young adult congregations, which rely heavily on larger, parent congregations for funding and worship space.

In the "Congregations that Get it" study, researchers studied three congregations from each of four faith traditions: Jewish, Muslim, Protestant, and Catholic. The twelve congregations were all urban and intergenerational; they were selected to represent a broad theological spectrum within each faith tradition. Study results are reported in detail in the book *Passing on the Faith: Transforming Traditions for the Next Generation of Jews, Christians, and Muslims.* The book also includes essays by practitioners from each religious tradition.

In reading these case studies together with survey research and interviews with practitioners, commonalities emerge across the divides of religious tradition and the spectrum of conservative/liberal theological beliefs. Some distinctions are also underscored, such as the unique role minority religions play in the identity development of young adherents. I touch on such distinctions, but I focus on the common threads, which I discuss in terms of four themes: identity, inclusion, inspiration, and innovation. Each theme is a crucial element of crafting a religious encounter that is authentic, accessible, and animating for a whole congregation, but particularly for young adults.

Identity

In an environment of spiritual tinkering, religious pluralism, and the declining significance of denominations, *more* attention to a congregation's identity, not less, is necessary. That is the conclusion of John Roberto (of LifelongFaith Associates) and Mike Hayes (author of *Googling God*). Their summary of best practices in young adult ministry argues it is "imperative" that congregations build community and encourage spiritual seeking "in the context of a clearly defined faith tradition" (2007, p 11). Congregational profiles confirm the importance of a clearly articulated collective identity: one grounded in a particular faith tradition but infused with a strong leader's vision and responsive to local contexts.

Some orthodox congregations have created a "niche" within their communities by encouraging inquiry while highlighting distinctive orthodox traditions. St. Ann's Parish, a Roman Catholic "mega-parish," has more than 28,000 members and seven weekly Masses. For young adult parishioners, much of the appeal comes from the church's emphasis on being unapologetically Catholic (Bruce 2010). Young adults are encouraged to attend Mass, go to confession, adhere to Church teachings on moral and social issues, and to spend time in the Perpetual Adoration Chapel, where parish members can pray and contemplate Scripture in the presence of the Eucharist 24 hours a day, year-round. Through small groups targeted toward "Twenty-Somethings," young adults have space to learn about the sacraments and church teachings and to encourage each other to rise to the challenge of embodying those teachings in a society that (in their view) encourages relativism.

Articulating a clear identity is one thing; communicating it is another. Evangelism is one model for communicating identity, but many liberal congregations avoid this framework. Instead, they think in terms of p. r. or "branding"—often with concerns about mixing the sacred with such calculatedly market-driven secular activity. Catholic theologian and Boston College professor Tim Muldoon (2008) argues that marketing spirituality is only a bad idea if what a ministry is "selling" is a lie. Effective marketing may not only attract newcomers but energize a congregation around a coherent vision of ministry.

Middle Collegiate Church (a progressive Protestant congregation in New York City) established a "brand" that both expresses and re-centers the congregation's identity (Yukich

34

2010). Four words appear prominently on the church website, ads, and documents: welcoming, inclusive, bold, and artistic. Church activities aim to embody these four concepts, from a rich musical program that includes regular performances by professional musicians to an active Gay, Lesbian, Bisexual, Transgender, and Intersex ministry. Younger members name its radical inclusivity and the emotional resonance of its music and arts as key to the congregation's appeal. Middle Church creates an authentic religious encounter for young adults not through young-adult-friendly programming (which it also has) but through opportunities to embody a clearly articulated vision of progressive religious community.

For religious minorities, congregations can play a distinctive role in personal identity formation. In the United States, most people perceive religious identity to be *achieved* or chosen rather than *ascribed*, or inherited. Empirical research suggests second-generation Muslims and Hindus apply this thinking to their faith as well (Warner 2002). Sociologist Lori Peek's (2005) interviews with Muslim college students propose a model of religious identity development moving from ascribed to chosen to publicly declared Islamic identity. At mosques in Detroit, second generation Muslim young adults report interest in distinguishing between practices that are general to Islam and those that are peculiar to ethnic or national cultures (Bagby 2007). Sometimes, they criticize their elders for failing to make such distinctions. Congregations that respond to this desire to choose one's religious identity can both guide and affirm young adults who navigate majority and minority cultural worlds.

Inclusion

Case studies report congregations that appeal to young adults are remarkably inclusive in three respects. They meet young adults where they are on their faith journey. They embody some form of diversity. And they invite young adults to leadership in congregational life.

Accessible: Accessible congregations "meet young adults where they are" in terms of religious knowledge and commitment (Belzer and Miller 2007). Today's young adults have diverse religious experiences. Almost half of 18-23-year-olds are disinvested from the customs of a particular denomination or faith tradition (Smith 2009). At the same time, many young adults are interested in interfaith exploration; one-third of 21-45-year-olds have attended services at a non-Christian place of worship (Wuthnow 2007). Along with diverse knowledge about religion, young adults often have anxiety about commitment—whether to a congregation, a romantic partner, or a job (Cunningham 2009). Many typical ways congregations build community with newcomers—joining small groups, serving on committees, making financial pledges—assume some basic knowledge and routine time commitments that prove to be barriers for younger adults.

From observations at twelve congregations, Belzer, et al. (2007) conclude that congregations that "get it" offer multiple points of entry into the life of the congregation: from worship services at various times during the week to spiritual retreats, Bible studies and adult education programs, social gatherings and opportunities to volunteer. They also avoid guilt trips or shame about young adults' sometimes-inconsistent attendance. Rabbi J. Rolondo Matalon of Congregation Bnai Jeshurun in Manhattan says that in a community, there has to be room for asymmetric exchanges of support (2007). His congregation aims to balance non-judgmental welcome with invitations to deeper engagement.

Diversity: Today's young adults are inclined to embrace diversity, or at least to honor individual differences, across a variety of measures. Compared to older cohorts, 18-29-year-olds support interracial dating, affirmative action, and gay marriage at higher rates (Smith 2009). While many young adults crave an inclusive, diverse faith community, that inclusivity is filtered through the lens of social and faith backgrounds. Inclusion may mean visible racial diversity, support for gay marriage and clergy, or allowing women to preach. What is largely consistent across congregations profiled is an *intentional* effort to embrace diversity in some form.

When New Life evangelical fellowship intentionally built a racially diverse congregation, they found themselves also attracting younger members (Cimino 2010). At The Crossing, a small "emergent" Christian church in Boston, progressive theology and a "radical welcome" are embodied by a congregation and leadership board with half straight and half gay, lesbian, queer, or transgendered people (Kaell 2010). At the Islamic Center of Southern California, the nine-person board includes four women, and some women choose to wear headscarves only during prayer (not during board meetings and social gatherings) (Belzer, et al 2007). These deliberate efforts convey powerful messages about what these congregations believe religious devotion looks like in the twenty-first century.

Leadership: All of the congregations in the ChangingSEA and Congregations That Get It studies include young adults in visible leadership roles within the church. Those roles involve varying degrees of commitment—from serving as occasional readers, musicians, and worship planners to chairing committees or serving as clergy. All Area Dulles Muslim Society (ADAMS) in Washington, DC, serves 10,000 Sunni participants. This large mosque deliberately seeks young adult leadership to ensure it will thrive in the long term; in the mid-2000s, its Sunday School director was 25, and all four executive officers were in their 30s (Belzer, et al. 2007).

Even in communities with particularly rapid young adult migration—such as college and university towns—congregations find ways to nurture young leaders. At St. Peter's Catholic Student Center in Waco, TX, that transient population of students *is* the core leadership of the congregation. A small group of older adults regularly joins students in worship. These adults see themselves in a supporting or mentoring role, appreciating the chance to see young adults test themselves by putting ambitious ministry ideas into practice (Palmer 2010). Brother John of Taizé (another Catholic ministry famous for its work with young adults) writes "when given responsibility, [young adults] very often rise to it" (2007, p 157). Relationships grounded in mutual trust are key to sharing the power and responsibilities that come with leadership roles.

Inspiration

Larry Braskamp studied faith-based colleges' investment in students' development. His advice to colleges also applies to congregations. He argues, "community is most effective in fostering student development when students regard it as a community of support and challenge" (2007, p 1). Many congregations that reach out to young adults begin and end their ministry with hospitality: providing a safe, non-judgmental environment. Hospitality is crucial, but those who study young adult development argue that young adults both expect and deserve more from religious communities. As Sharon Daloz-Parks would say, they deserve mentors who will support them through crises and encourage them to dream worthwhile dreams for their future.

Three congregational "best practices" are particularly inspiring for young adults: dynamic, participatory, and emotionally engaging worship; invested clergy; and opportunities to serve. Young adults are often associated with "contemporary" styles of worship. Wuthnow (2007) and Flory and Miller (2008) argue that many of the features associated with contemporary worship—such as praise music and an informal setting—most appeal to the Baby Boomer generation. Hackett (2010) finds 18-29-year-olds report valuing traditional and contemporary worship about evenly. More important to them is worship that engages both brain and body (Flory and Miller 2008). It is no coincidence that congregations with active young adult membership often emphasize arts and music. Young adults (21-45) who pray or meditate regularly are more likely to do so while listening to music than while reading the Bible or a devotional guide (Wuthnow 2007). Compared to older adults, they draw fewer boundaries between secular and sacred music. Whereas older adults are more likely to report being inspired by "church music"—classical, traditional hymns, and even Christian pop music, younger adults find spiritual inspiration from music they listen to everyday (Wuthnow 2007). For more on congregational worship styles and practices, see Royle's report "FACTs on Worship: 2010."

Clergy have an especially important role as mentors. At Consolidated Baptist, an African American Southern Baptist Congregation in Lexington, KY, Pastor Richard Gaines tells young adults to "Think Big!" (Bower 2010). He has ambitions for young adults in his community, especially vulnerable African American college students who may be struggling to balance work, school, and family obligations. For African American and Latino young adults, religious congregations can be a source of strength and encouragement in the face of social and economic pressures (Warner 2002; Owens 2010). Rev. Gaines spends time at the local university campus, meeting young people, listening to their stories, and inviting them to worship. Inspired by his passion, Consolidated Baptist now offers a weekly "Real Talk" Bible study for young adults, includes young adults in leadership positions, and incorporates hip-hop music into worship. Other congregations with large, diverse young adult programming tell similar stories of clergy with vision who get the ball rolling.

Finally, congregations also give young adults opportunities to reach out to others, whether through evangelism, volunteer work, social justice advocacy, or experiences like short-term mission trips. From a developmental perspective, young adults are deeply self-focused: they are learning who they are and what kind of adults they hope to be. This does not mean they are selfish; indeed, for many, one sign of maturity is attending to the needs of others (Arnett 2004). Congregations make it easy for young adults to put that interest into practice through social outreach programs.

Innovation

The 1,200 members at non-denominational New Life Fellowship in Queens, New York, are adept spiritual tinkerers. Leaders mix an evangelical mission and theology with neo-monastic and contemplative practices to foster an "emotionally healthy spirituality." Sociologist Richard Cimino (2010) argues that this ability to maintain a core identity while innovating in non-core aspects of church life may be key to sustainable long-term growth for any congregation.

Pastor Carol Howard Merritt makes a similar point in *Tribal Church: Ministering to the Missing Generation.* She says congregations that want to build strong intergenerational relationships should bear in mind Diana Butler Bass' distinction between *tradition* and *customs.* Traditions ground a search for truth or meaning through continuity with historical ways of knowing and practicing faith. Customs are the things congregations (and people) do simply because that's how they have always done them. They make up the "invisible rule book" of congregational life, and Merritt argues that customs can and should be changed if congregations hope to welcome new members into their communities. She cautions that many congregations eagerly add young adults to committees in the hopes of relieving burned-out older leaders; fewer congregations are able to let go of customs enough to allow young leaders to shape the direction of the church.

Successful innovation is attentive to a congregation's core identity and the dynamic social contexts in which that congregation is embedded. Thus, a program founded in one congregational setting may be inappropriate or require adaptation for another. Below is a partial list of innovative ways congregations have responded to the needs of a young adult population:

Linking the Social and Spiritual
Many young adult-focused ministries blur the lines between the sacred and the social. Those lines exist for a reason, but

well-considered changes to the ways congregations use physical space or time events can highlight the continuity of the sacred and social functions of congregational life. At St. Peter's Catholic Student Center, students hang out in the space for hours, chatting, doing homework, or watching movies; when it is time to worship, students "fluidly transition" within the same space (Palmer 2010). In Detroit, young adult Muslims feel greater connection to their mosques if they see mosques as a place to make friends and play as well as learn and pray (Bagby 2007).

Some congregations take the sacred to secular spaces. The Catholic Diocese of Chicago has popularized the practice of "Theology on Tap:" evenings at a bar or restaurant where keynote speakers address matters of faith, from vocations and moral puzzles to Catholic social teaching (Cusick and Devries 2001). The basic premise of Theology on Tap – conversations about faith in a neutral, sociable environment for people who may be wary of religious institutions – has been adopted by diverse (largely Christian) traditions. They have also adapted the event, for example traditions that disapprove of alcohol or want to welcome people in recovery may shift venues to a coffee shop.

Informal Networks
Congregations are great at creating small groups or programs to cater to special needs; young adult ministries often take the form of named programs, like the humorous "Bagels and Bible" study group or the straightforward "Jewish Young Adults of Hoboken/Hudson." Clay United Methodist took a different approach, focusing on relationships and face-to-face networking (Farrell 2010). At Clay, young adult gatherings over coffee or dinner are "obsessively informal." Events are not named. There is no agenda. Dates and times are not simply announced on Facebook or in the church bulletin with an open invitation. Instead, the pastor or host invites younger adults personally. Information about events circulates through email or word of mouth. The obsessive informality can be reassuring for a group unable to make or uncomfortable with

time-intensive commitments. The personal touch connects with young adults' craving to feel like a vital part of a community. Though the focus is on quality of relationships, not quantity, these methods have grown Clay's young adult population to about 15 percent of regular church participants.

Rethinking Social Media
Congregations wanting to engage younger adults almost certainly need a basic digital literacy and some kind of web presence to be taken seriously. Maintaining an up-to-date website with a calendar of events keeps congregants of all ages in the loop. Many churches also post sermons or podcasts online; a few even maintain a primarily online presence. Revolution Church, (www.revolutionnyc.com), with branches in Atlanta and Brooklyn, meets weekly for services (at a music venue in Brooklyn), but its largest ministry is a podcast broadcasting sermons to a weekly audience of thousands. For more on congregations and technology, see Thumma (2011) for an overview of US congregations' technology use; Farrell (2011) for a comparison of conservative and mainline Protestant congregations' web use; and Miller, Mundy, and Hill (2013) or Bobkowski and Pearce (2011) for research on young adults, religion, and social media usage.

Media-savvy congregations have found the Internet and social media to be a double-edged sword. In D.C., young adults use Facebook to learn about upcoming Catholic events across the city (Garces-Foley 2010). They can also check Facebook to find out who plans to attend or not. Some single young adults admit they peruse the guest list for attractive prospects, hoping to meet like-minded singles. A counter-productive cycle begins, with invitees waiting to see what others will do, then ultimately deciding not to go when the "yes" column is low (which may be because peers are also playing the wait-and-see game).

Rabbis Josh Feigelson and Scott Aaron urge congregations to reframe their thinking when it comes to technology and social media. Rather than asking how congregations can *use* technology to reach young adults, they say, ask: "How do developments in technology change what it means to be an emerging adult?" (Feigelson and Aaron, forthcoming). In other words, technology is not only a tool, it's a social force that shapes daily life. For young adults, technology plays a role in key developmental tasks, from finding romantic partners to maintaining friendships to searching for meaningful work. To use technology judiciously, congregations must consider how technology shapes human relationships – and what that means for building community as a congregation.

Extra-congregational ventures
Many innovative practices in young adult ministries take place outside congregational contexts: on college campuses, in mission fields around the world, through business ventures, or through geographically dispersed social networks (to name a few). Guides to campus ministry abound; an Amazon search for "college ministry" produces nearly 4,500 results. Many include advice for partnering with local congregations to foster intergenerational connections. Religious programs modeled after the Peace Corps or AmeriCorps place young people in faith-based social service agencies or mission fields around the globe. Some recruit local congregations to provide housing, mentors, and a spiritual home during volunteers' stay.

Faith-driven business ventures apply free market enterprise to spiritual purposes. National Community Church in Washington, D.C., owns and operates Ebenezer's, a coffeehouse "with a cause." The café has free Wi-Fi, meeting spaces, and live music events, serving as a community hub and hangout space (http://ebenezerscoffeehouse.com/). Whether or not customers become church members, the coffee shop serves the church's mission by offering a calm, welcoming space in a fast-paced city, investing in fair trade products, and using proceeds to support social outreach programs.

Reboot is a multi-city non-profit venture with the goal of helping new generations "grapple with questions of Jewish identity, community, and meaning" (www.rebooters.net). An annual summit provides a focal point for a broad network of Jewish and non-Jewish artists, academics, social activists, and politicians to maintain conversation and jump-start local events, art installations, and other creative ventures, such as the Idelsohn Society for Musical Preservation, which curates a digital archive of Jewish music, releasing albums with engrossing liner notes about the creation of songs and artists' lives (www.rebootstereophonic.com).

Conclusion

Despite widespread indifference to religious organizations among young adults, recent research documents many effective congregational responses to this population's changing social worlds. Appropriately, these responses are as varied as the population of young adults itself. Having a clear identity, inspiring community members, and innovative worship and programs are all characteristics of thriving congregations, no matter the age of members. Certain practices are especially resonant for young adults: inclusion of diverse voices; invitation to share leadership responsibilities; cultivating mentoring relationships; blending the social and sacred functions of congregational life. These are just a few of the ways congregations create a welcoming community for young spiritual tinkerers.

Though research on young adults' religiosity has expanded rapidly in the past ten years, some aspects of young adults' religious engagement remain cloudy. The case studies in this review all depict thriving congregations in urban settings, neglecting smaller and suburban or rural congregations. They are also success stories, and clearly not all congregations are succeeding with young adults. It is not enough to contrast success stories with all other churches; failure is different from inadequacy. Future research should consider whether and how congregations fail young adults.

Existing research has made some effort to examine differences in terms of racial/ethnic background and religious tradition, though much more could be done. More importantly, research overwhelmingly focuses on college-educated or - attending young adults. Undoubtedly, these young people can benefit from and offer much to congregations. Yet evidence suggests congregations can be an even greater lifeline for marginalized young adults. The barriers to religious participation are higher for these groups. While practitioners may specialize in vulnerable populations, more systematic research could provide key insights into ways congregations can best engage vulnerable young adults – such as those who have "graduated" from foster care or the juvenile justice system, runaways, or those living with mental or physical disabilities without the support of strong family networks.

Congregations that fear that churches are failing to reach young adults have reason to worry. The customs and rhythms of congregational life are designed for stability and continuity with the past; they are not well suited to dramatic, rapid transition. Young adults today spend long stretches of their life in an unsettled state marked by uncertainty, instability, and hope. Congregations that cannot adapt to minister to a mobile population of spiritual tinkerers have little hope of convincing young people that religious institutions have any relevance for their lives, now or in the future. The uncertain futures congregations now face have inspired both researchers and faith communities to better understand and respond to young adults' religious beliefs and yearnings. The body of research reveals that, like their target population, congregational efforts to engage young adults show both vulnerability and promise.

LiErin Probasco completed a Ph.D. in sociology at Princeton University where she served as associate director at the Center for the Study of Religion. She has also taught at Kean University in New Jersey, Lutheran Theological Seminary in Philadelphia, Union Presbyterian Seminary in Richmond, Perkins School of Theology at Southern Methodist University and Andover Newton Theological School. She has served as young adult ministries intern at the United Church of Christ headquarters in Cleveland and as a research staff member at the Community Development Institute in East Palo Alto, California.

References

Arnett, Jeffrey Jensen. 2004. *Emerging adulthood: The winding road from the late teens through the twenties*: Oxford University Press, USA.

Astin, Alexander W., Helen S. Astin, and Jennifer A. Lindholm. 2005. "The Spiritual Life of College Students: A National Study of College Students' Search for Meaning and Purpose." Los Angeles: Higher Education Research Institute (HERI), University of California, Los Angeles.

Bagby, Ihsan. 2007. "Second-generation Muslim immigrants in Detroit mosques: The second generation's search for their place and identity in the American mosque." Pp. 218-244 in *Passing on the faith: transforming traditions for the next generation of Jews, Christians, and Muslims*, edited by SM Heft and L James. New York: Fordham University Press.

Belzer, Tobin, Richard W. Flory, Nadia Roumani, and Brie Loskota. 2007. "Congregations that get it: Understanding religious identities in the next generation." Pp. 115-134 in *Passing on the faith: transforming traditions for the next generation of Jews, Christians, and Muslims*, edited by SM Heft and L James. New York: Fordham University Press.

Belzer, Tobin, and Donald Earl Miller. 2007. *Synagogues that Get It: How Jewish Congregations are Engaging Young Adults*: S3K Synagogue Studies Institute.

Bobkowski, Piotr and Lisa D. Pearce. 2011. "Baring Their Souls in Online Profiles or Not? Religious Self-Disclosure in Social Media." Journal for the Scientific Study of Religion. 50(4):744-762.

Bower, Walt. 2010. "Consolidated Baptist Church." in *Changing SEA Project*, edited by Kathleen Garces-Foley. Washington, DC: The Institute for Policy Research & Catholic Studies, Catholic University of America.

Braskamp, Larry A. 2007. "Fostering Religious and Spiritual Development of Students during College." SSRC Forum on the Religious Engagements of American Undergraduates. www.religion.ssrc.org/reforum. Accessed 3/1/2013.

Brother John of Taizé. 2007. "A Spiritual crossroads of Europe: The Taizé community's adventure with the young " Pp. 147-161 in *Passing on the faith: transforming traditions for the next generation of Jews, Christians, and Muslims*, edited by SM Heft and L James. New York: Fordham University Press.

Bruce, Tricia. 2010. "Engaging Young Adults at a Catholic Mega-parish." in *Changing SEA Project*, edited by Kathleen Garces-Foley. Washington, DC: The Institute for Policy Research & Catholic Studies, Catholic University of America.

Cimino, Richard. 2010. "Diversity and spirituality drive young adults at New Life Fellowship." in *Changing SEA Project*, edited by Kathleen Garces-Foley. Washington, DC: The Institute for Policy Research & Catholic Studies, Catholic University of America.

Clydesdale, Tim, Kathleen Garces-Foley, Anthony J. Pogorelc, and James Youniss. 2010. "The Changing Spirituality of Emerging Adults Project." The Institute for Policy Research & Catholic Studies.

Farrell, Justin. 2011. "The Divine Online: Civic Organizing, Identity Building, and Internet Fluency among Different Religious Groups." *Journal of Media and Religion.*

----. 2010. "Clay United Methodist Church." in *Changing SEA Project*, edited by Kathleen Garces-Foley. Washington, DC: The Institute for Policy Research & Catholic Studies, Catholic University of America.

Flory, Richard, and Donald Miller. 2008. *Finding faith: The spiritual quest of the post-boomer generation*: Rutgers University Press.

Garces-Foley, Kathleen. 2010. "Engaging Young Adult Catholics in D.C." in *Changing SEA Project*, edited by Kathleen Garces-Foley. Washington, DC: The Institute for Policy Research & Catholic Studies, Catholic University of America.

Hackett, Conrad. 2010. "Emerging Adult Participation in Congregations." in *Changing SEA Project*, edited by Tim Clydesdale. Washington, DC: The Institute for Policy Research & Catholic Studies, Catholic University of America.

Hayes, Michael. 2007. *Googling God: The Religious Landscape of People in their 20s and 30s.* Mahwah, NJ: Paulist Press/Busted Halo Books.

Kaell, Hillary. 2010. "The Crossing: Worship, Community, and Action in Emergent Episcopal Ministry." in *Changing SEA Project*, edited by Kathleen Garces-Foley. Washington, DC: The Institute for Policy Research & Catholic Studies, Catholic University of America.

Lugo, Luis. 2012. ""Nones" on the Rise: One-in-Five Adults Have No Religious Affiliation." Pew Research Center's Forum on Religion & Public Life.

Matalon, Rabbi J. Rolando. 2007. "Bj: A portrait of a revitalized synagogue." Pp. 125-134 in *Passing on the faith: transforming traditions for the next generation of Jews, Christians, and Muslims*, edited by SM Heft and L James. New York: Fordham University Press.

Mayrl, Damon, and Jeremy E Uecker. 2011. "Higher Education and Religious Liberalization among Young Adults." *Social Forces* 90:181-208.

Merritt, Carol Howard. 2007. *Tribal church: Ministering to the missing generation*: Alban Institute.

Miller, Brian J., Peter Mundey, and Jonathan P. Hill. 2013. "Faith in the Age of Facebook: Exploring the Links Between Religion and Social Network Site Membership and Use." *Sociology of Religion.*

Palmer, Ashley. 2010. "St. Peter's Catholic Student Center." in *Changing SEA Project*, edited by Kathleen Garces-Foley. Washington, DC: The Institute for Policy Research & Catholic Studies, Catholic University of America.

Parks, Sharon Daloz. 2000. *Big questions, worthy dreams: Mentoring young adults in their search for meaning, purpose, and faith*: Jossey-Bass San Francisco, CA.

Pond, Allison, Gregory Smith, and Scott Clement. 2010. "Religion Among the Millennials: Less Religiously Active Than Older Americans, But Fairly Traditional In Other Ways." Washington, DC: Pew Research Center

Roberto, John, and Mike Hayes. 2007. "Best Practices in Young Adult Faith Formation." *Lifelong Faith - LifelongFaith Associates.*

Royle, Marjorie. 2010. "FACTS on Worship:2010." Faith Communities Today. www.faithcommunitiestoday.org.

Thumma, Scott. 2011. "Virtually Religious: Technology and Internet Use in American Congregations." Faith Communities Today. www.hartfordinstitute.org/research/technology-Internet-use.html. Accessed 3/1/2013.

Smith, Christian. 2009. *Souls in transition: The religious and spiritual lives of emerging adults*. New York: Oxford University Press USA.

Ukeles, Jacob B., Ron Miller, and Pearl Beck. 2006. *Young Jewish Adults in the United States Today.* New York: American Jewish Committee.

Winston, Diane. 2007. "Teach your children well: Closing observations on constructing religious identity in the next generation." Pp. 264-274 in *Passing on the faith: transforming traditions for the next generation of Jews, Christians, and Muslims*, edited by SM Heft and L James. New York: Fordham University Press.

Wuthnow, Robert. 2007. *After the baby boomers: How twenty- and thirty-somethings are shaping the future of American religion.* Princeton, NJ: Princeton University Press.

Yukich, Grace. 2010. "Middle Collegiate Church." in *Changing SEA Project*, edited by Kathleen Garces-Foley. Washington, DC: The Institute for Policy Research & Catholic Studies, Catholic University of America.

Chapter 3
ChristWay Community Church
Ooltewah, Tennessee

By Carole Kilcher

ChristWay Community Church (CWCC) is located at 6201 Mountain View Road in Ooltewah, Tennessee, not far from the Georgia state line. The name reflects the church's mission to "follow Christ and walk in his Way." It was first organized as Central Baptist Church with 53 members in 1887. After several relocations, in 2001 the congregation moved to Ooltewah.

Ooltewah is a suburban community in Hamilton County outside Chattanooga. The church building faces Interstate 75, the major highway between Knoxville and Atlanta. As of 2011, Ooltewah's population was 7,623. Since 2000 it has had a population growth of 34 percent. The Little Debbie snack cake plant and Blue Planet factory have been located here for many years. More recently, Volkswagen moved part of its Passat manufacturing operation to the area. In addition, the Amazon.Com facilities are now fully operating at nearby Enterprise South Industrial Park.

The church is located next door to Ooltewah High School with an enrollment of 1,242 during the 2011-2012 school year. It has an active ministry at the high school. More important to this case study is the fact that there are five colleges and universities with over 20,900 full-time students within 16 miles of the church. Three miles away in Collegedale is Southern Adventist University with 2,273 students. Chattanooga State Community College is nine miles away with an enrollment of 4,410. The University of Tennessee at Chattanooga with 8,652 students is 13 miles away. About 15 miles away in Cleveland, Tennessee, is Lee University with an enrollment of 3,586 and Cleveland State Community College with 2,031 students.

CWCC has a pastoral staff of four, including Lead Pastor John Waters, Executive Pastor Kevin Preston, Worship Leader Matt Coleman and Minister to Students Matt Moore. They have three support staff. Affiliated with the Southern Baptist Convention, the church is "Bible-focused" and led by a group of lay elders, not the pastor alone or an elected body.

The church is housed in a remodeled, repurposed industrial building where Arnold Palmer golf clubs were once manufactured. A portion of the warehouse is unfinished but available for expansion. Although connected to completed hallways, the vast expanse and cement floor is an alternative area used occasionally for events that are not appropriate for carpeted floors.

A number of cozy areas are set apart for fellowship and ministry. These include, but are not limited to the following: sitting areas with couches, lamps, and tables in various places throughout; two Bistros, one of which is specifically for those in grades 9-12; the ChristWay Theater; a café, the upstairs Attic; the Living Room, which is a prayer room with soft lights and more couches and chairs; as well as the Worship Center.

In the large foyer there is a square information desk called "Connection Central". A visitor can learn more about the church here. There are a variety of brochures and informational papers laid out on the counter. First time visitors are given a steel water bottle with the church website embossed on it and a ticket for a free breakfast at the Bistro, where coffee and breakfast foods are available.

The Worship Center

Entering the Worship Center one observes movable padded chairs and a stage with no decorations. Two large video screens flank either side of the stage. Theater-like stage lights allow for change in color and other lighting effects. A professional camera is on a tripod on a platform along the right side of congregation facing the stage. Sound boards and video control equipment are housed in the back. A roving camera person captures on-stage action.

During the school year, three services are held to accommodate worshipers. The philosophy is that if there is room to park and if people do not feel cramped in worship, they will come. Additionally the various children's classrooms can only legally hold so many individuals at any given time.

CWCC makes a point of being casual and accepting. Attendees may wear whatever makes them comfortable, and are free to bring their coffee into the worship center. They may choose their own seat or have an usher assist them. If it is raining, volunteers meet cars with umbrellas, making sure everyone gets inside as dry as possible.

An Account of One Worship Service

A video counts down seven minutes on both large screens to the minute the service begins with music from a band. The instruments of the band include a keyboard, four electric guitars and a drum set. Those players are joined by one male lead vocalist and two female back-up singers. Members of the band must audition for a position in the band. The music is contemporary, loud and lively. The church once tried to have another room where the music was streamed and volume could be controlled. They tried it for a few weeks but hardly anyone came. Those in attendance participate in singing and praising the Lord.

James Howard and Brian Smith, wearing yellow t-shirts inscribed with the CWCC motto, "Changing the way you think about church," give the announcements in a pre-recorded video called "In The Know." They banter back and forth with good humor while outlining what is coming up during the coming week and preparing the congregation for the important items in the immediate weeks ahead. There are no church bulletins but each week's "In the Know" is immediately posted on the church website.

The lights change and focus on Pastor Waters who this week is sitting on a stool. He wears very casual clothes. He announces that his notes are on the cell phone Bible "You Version" if anyone wants to follow along.

He bases his sermon on Acts 9 and 1 and 2 Timothy, talking about the importance of a church's responsibility to make disciples. Making disciples, he says, takes time but is the responsibility of every partner of the congregation, not just the pastors and elders.

He asks the congregation to stand if any comment he is about to make applies to them. First he asks how many, when in an elevator, prefer to look at the lights denoting which floor it is on rather than the others in the elevator. He then asks how many like cats. After several icebreaking questions such as these, the audience is responding. Then Pastor Waters asks how many gave their hearts to the Lord at a big Billy Graham crusade or any other large public evangelistic meeting. A few respond. Finally he asks, "How many can name one or two people who invested in your life and led you to the Lord?" Hundreds rise. Pastor Waters concludes, "We must invest in others' lives if we are going to be a disciple-making church."

Interview with Youth/Young Adult Pastor

On June 6, 2012, the author interviewed Matt Moore, CWCC's youth pastor, who oversees the college program. He relies heavily on mature Christians who volunteer to lead out in the Life Groups for this age group. Young adult Life Group leaders work closely with Pastor Moore; however, his primary responsibility is to the high-school age group.

During the interview he told me that the Worship Center seats approximately 500 worshipers. The annual growth for the last five years has been noticeable. When Pastor John Waters became the lead pastor, there were 100 or fewer individuals attending on any given Sunday. Three years later, when he joined the team, 300 individuals were involved. Pastor Moore estimated that there are now more than 800 regular attendees and visitors seeking fellowship and worship at CWCC.

Pastor Moore and his team work to transition high school seniors into the church's young adult-college age group. The goal is to focus ministry on life-stages through circles of fellowship and Bible study. For example, one of the high school girls' groups is co-led by a mature Christian and a young adult as a role model to the younger girls. In 2012, a mission trip to Haiti sponsored by CWCC was an enriching experience for high school seniors, allowing them to get away from their norm and obtain a wider perspective.

One member whose children are in the high school age group said, "Frankly, my kids are the reason I come to this church. They want to come to all the activities and be with their friends. I guess I would come if they didn't because I am involved, but some Sundays I know I would be tempted to sleep in."

Many young adult ministries struggle with moving people from one stage to another. A ministry that begins as a young adult ministry changes as its members change, becoming a family-oriented church, then a church of older people who are struggling to reach young adults in its own turn. CWCC's solution to this is to maintain age limits. A member named Amy said that she had recently been "kicked out" of the college age group that she had attended for a long time. "Well, not kicked out, really. The church just changed the age from 19 to 29, and made the top age limit 25. I guess they knew that some of us would never leave if they didn't." Amy shared that she loved the group study and its activities but now that she is married she volunteers in the children's areas at church and enjoys that also. In her opinion, young adults stay with this congregation because they are involved in its running and leadership.

Pastor Matt stated that the age range was changed to 18 to 25 because of their philosophy that their job is to help individuals make a healthy transition into their next stage of life. Whereas someone may still be in college at age 29 or beyond, they have (or should have) moved to the next stage of life. They may have a spouse, a child or children and their relationship with Jesus and personal goals are usually different from that of an 18-year-old. They have no record of the exact percentage of the general membership that are between the ages of 18 and 29.

Life Groups are key to the young adult ministry at CWCC. In addition, they also take advantage of opportunities for group projects, retreats and the Passion Conference, which in 2012 was held January 2-5 in nearby Atlanta. During the summer months, the young adults meet for Bible Study or just to "hang out" at the homes of Joey and Tiffanie Wilson and Justin and Leslie Kilgore.

CWCC also believes in learning by watching. When the college-age group meets in the home of married couples who hold jobs, they learn by observation what their life can look like in the future. "The one thing we can be sure of is that if there is food they will come!" exclaims Matt with a smile. They are encouraged not only to eat and moot but to learn of venues where their talents and spiritual gifts can be used. Pastor Moore said, "We set expectations for them that church is a place to belong and serve."

The thing all young adults have in common is the desire to have a place to connect, to belong, and to have an experience that meets their needs in worship. Building relationships with mature Christians helps them see what they can have in the next stage of their life.

Because young adults are busy with school, work and other obligations Matt described how they are working to have a Life Group in every community near the college campuses that the church serves. During the summer months Life Groups do not meet regularly but a listing of times young adults will meet is listed on the website. The young adults who are able are encouraged to participate in one of the missions outside their comfort zone during the summer. When asked about the budget for his area of ministry he told me that they were not willing to give out that information.

Pastor Moore concluded by saying, "The leadership is not striving to have CWCC become a mega church where nobody knows your name. God is doing scary things with the growth of this church and our job is to be ready for what He is doing next."

On-Site Interviews of Young Adult Worshipers

Having visited before, but wanting to learn more, I attended CWCC again in June of 2012. I was very impressed when Beth, the executive administrative assistant of CWCC, spoke to me by name even though we had only met once before, when I came to interview the pastor.

On this day, I went to the Bistro and elected to visit with a young adult who was sitting alone at one of the tables. She had the black shirt on with the motto of the church: "Changing the way you think about church." I asked her if she was in the college-age Life Group. She replied that she is 22 and meets in a group at another church. Interested, I asked, "What draws you to this church enough to keep coming back when you are in a group at another congregation?"

She replied, "It is because this church is different from all the others. I like the band instead of a choir. I like how Pastor John's messages speak to issues I am dealing with or need to hear. He encourages us to use our cell phones for the Bible passages using the 'You Version' app and even puts his sermon notes up on You Version 'Live' so we can follow along."

After thanking her for her time I visited the "Attic" where the high school classrooms are located. It is up several flights of steps. The walls are painted black with a montage of texts and sayings written in white paint on the first landing. At the top landing one sees a large room with a stage. That day chairs were arranged in small groups along the edge of the room. Smaller classrooms were evident down a long hallway.

I chatted with a 30-something man who told me he was the teacher for the Grade 11 boys. I asked him why their high school youth ministry is separated by both grade and gender. He said they find that boys open up much more easily when not mixed in with girls. The same is true that the girls open up among other girls, although not as much as the boys do when taught alone. The separation by grade is because they have found that these are the times when their life stage is in transition. This is the way the adult teacher/mentor can be a friend to them, guide them and give instruction in what they specifically need at that stage of their life. The goal is to transition them into the next stage in healthy ways and keeping them in the church as they become young adults. This particular teacher suggested that in his experience he had never seen a youth/young adult ministry program in a church as effective as this at CWCC.

I went to the Worship Center for the 10:30 service. There were young adults sitting near me. There are no young small children in the worship center as they are being served by volunteers in the Big Wazoo or Tree House. At worship, high school teens, young adults and young married couples are in abundance. In stark contrast to most Christian churches, an individual with gray hair is definitely in the minority at CWCC. The congregation at this particular service was made up almost entirely of whites with few minorities. The service is in English.

During the video, "In the Know", this week only Jack Howard gave the announcements. If he is reading it is off a teleprompter, as he speaks with rapid pace and looks straight at the audience. He always wears one of the church-identifying yellow t-shirts. In preparation for Father's Day, he asked for pictures of fathers and sons. He said, "If you have one of you and your son or you and your father on your phone, you can send it right now to pics@christway.org."

In another highlighted announcement, Jack noted the baptism and cook-out was next Sunday. In other matters, materials for the mission trip to St. Louise for college age youth, need to be turned in next week, the flip flops, soccer balls and underwear for the Honduras mission trip are also due by next week. He referred us to a table in the foyer near Connection Central that was displaying items as examples of what was needed.

He said if any Life Group wanted to have something special for their group to do together this summer CWCC would be passing out popsicles at the Collegedale fireworks being held this year on July 3. He asked everyone to wear their CWCC t-shirts. He talked about different ways to deliver prayer requests to those in prayer ministry. These included a phone number, a website and, within the" You Version" Bible App., a place to send prayer requests from one's phone.

A short video was played, leading up to Pastor John's sermon series in the books of Timothy and Titus. When the lights came up, John was seated in one of four chairs at a very nice dining room table with a basket of bread in the center. John's sermons are archived on the CWCC website in both audio and video format. They can be downloaded or listened to online. One can also subscribe to them as a podcast in ITunes so they update automatically.

Today's sermon highlighted the four chairs around the table as representing the four stages of church life leading to one who becomes a mature Christian serving and seeking the lost. He hung a church t-shirt over the first seeker chair then proceeded to explain how it was important that an individual keep growing in Christ and moving around the table to become a mature Christian who disciples another. (See

sermon video at
http://christwaychurch.org/media.php?pageID=53)

Becoming a CWCC "Partner" is a Formal Process

People who join and regularly attend CWCC are known as "partners" rather than members. In order to join the church, one is invited to attend the "Discover ChristWay" new partner orientation. These orientation classes are held at different times throughout the year. A booklet outlining CWCC's distinctive mission, function, values, vision, strategy, theology and membership covenant can be found on ChristWay website. The document also outlines the covenants of the "Baptist Faith and Message" as given by the Southern Baptist Convention on pages 10-16. After conversion and baptism by immersion, a "Partnership Covenant" is signed. It is simple, asking the new "partner" to follow Christ by doing what the Bible asks all believers to do. This is outlined on pages 17-19 of the orientation booklet. Many have been "plugged in" to a Life Group and are already serving in some volunteer role before their baptism.

On-site Observation of Baptism in a Pond

There is a pond in front of the church. A stone baptistry has been formed on the edge of the pond that can be filled with fresh water on the days when a baptism is held. Typically, two outside baptisms are held during the warmer months. For the one held during the winter a portable baptistry is set up inside. On June 17 at 5 p.m. (Father's Day), the first of the 2012 baptismal events was held. It was much anticipated and well announced in advance both on the web, on the announcement sheets that are in bathrooms and during regular announcement time prior to worship. Baptism at CWCC is a celebration. Worshipers were reminded to bring lawn chairs or blankets and a 2-liter bottle of their favorite soda. A cookout would precede the baptism and there would be inflatable's and other activities for the kids.

CWCC baptisms are an event for all ages. During the services in the Worship Center, I had not been able to observe parents with their children due to the intentional separation of adults and the smaller children. Today, I saw a huge number of families with young children. This was particularly apparent where two large inflatable's had been set up especially for the younger children to enjoy.

When I went inside the church foyer to use the restroom, I noticed six college-age adults sprawled on couches and the floor having a serious discussion. I wished I might listen in, but did not feel that my timing was appropriate. When I exited the church, Beth told me that 21 individuals were to be baptized that day.

Over the loud speakers came the word that we were to line up to pick up our food. Those being baptized were reminded to meet in the Bistro at 6:15. The church supplied hotdogs already in buns with the typical fixings, coleslaw, a small bag of chips, and a Little Debbie snack cake. (The Little Debbie factory is located in this community.)

At 6:30 the candidates for baptism made two lines. Those who did not formerly have one of the church's t-shirts were now wearing one in blue that had been given to them at the meeting in the Bistro. Other than that identification they each wore what they chose in which to be baptized. Pastor Waters offered prayer and explained that the angels in Heaven were celebrating and that we should be too. He encouraged us to clap and cheer. There are steps at each end of the baptismal leading into the water and first a candidate on the right and then a candidate on the left were baptized.

There were hundreds gathered on the shore and after each candidate emerged from the water a cheer and much clapping ensued. Two young adults were among those baptized. Their college and Life Group leaders were named by the pastor during their introduction.

Summary

The appeal for young adults at this church is easy to understand when considering the myriads of ways the church gives opportunity to engage them. High school youth are intentionally transitioned into the young adult groups, whether they go to college or not. The philosophy that this is a place to "come as you are" with no need to dress up gives young adults a place with a Starbucks-like feel where they know they will be accepted and find a place to belong. The fact that coffee, breakfast items and fellowship are on-site regardless of which worship service one chooses to attend is an added plus. Belonging is also encouraged in smaller Life Groups that meet during the week in the casual environment of homes of young married couples.

The motto "Changing The Way People Think About Church" embossed on t-shirts that identify CWCC partners is another way young adults feel included within a larger context. In addition CWCC's ministry functions, not the gospel, have adapted to changing times. This is evident in the pastors' reference to Facebook or Twitter, the importance of having a media specialist on staff which enables an always-up-to-date website, and use of current technologies which include, but are not limited to, the video countdown and video announcement period each week, podcasts, the use of the "You Vision" Bible site for pastor's notes, and video archives if a message is missed.

The contemporary nature of the music and the worship service is not all that different from other congregations who have chosen that worship style genre. It is this researcher's opinion that when compared to other churches in the area, ChristWay Community Church has a reputation for effective strategies for engaging young adults.

Carole Kilcher is an adjunct faculty member in the social work and family studies department at Southern Adventist University in Collegedale, Tennessee. She served for a number of years as associate director of the Institute of Church Ministry at Andrews University and an instructor in the communication department.

References

ChristWay Church website: http://christwaychurch.org

Background information:
www.bestplaces.net/city/tennessee/ooltewah

Chapter 4
The Church of Jesus Christ of Latter-day Saints
Herriman, Utah

By Emily Layton

"God reaches into every part of our lives," asserts Danielle, a member of the Herriman Young Single Adult Ward of The Church of Jesus Christ of Latter-day Saints. (The names of members have been changed to protect their privacy.) The Herriman Young Single Adult (YSA) Ward, located in a suburban Utah community, is a robust gathering place for more than 200 young men and women ages 18–30. In a modern culture where religious beliefs and traditions are often criticized and moral values often mocked, it is worth exploring a congregation where young adults feel connected to God. What draws them to participate with this group?

Demographics and History of Young Single Adult Congregations

This congregation (or "ward") consists of young, unmarried adults from Herriman, Utah. Herriman is a rapidly growing city of approximately 29,000 predominantly white middle-class residents located 20 miles from Salt Lake City at the southwest edge of the Salt Lake valley. A 2011 survey showed the median resident age for Herriman was 24.7, and according to 2011 U.S. Census data, the estimated median household income was $77, 800. Herriman is 9.1 square miles in area and is primarily a residential community, with a library, a recreation center, a grocery store, several doctors' offices, and a number of restaurants and small businesses. The city was founded in 1851 by Latter-day Saint (LDS) pioneers, suggesting deep historical roots for the LDS Church in this community. The building where the ward meets is a modern structure, but a historical marker on the property identifies it as the site of the original rock church building erected in 1879. It is one of nearly a dozen LDS meetinghouses in Herriman.

The LDS Church (sometimes called the Mormon Church) divides members into wards based on geographic location (in some areas "branches" are smaller groups of members). Each is presided over by a bishop, usually a married man from the congregation who serves as a lay minister for a few years. Members meet weekly for worship services and also gather regularly for other service and social activities. The LDS Church has approximately 29,014 wards and branches (smaller congregations) worldwide. (2012 General Conference Statistical Report) Wards are aggregated into "stakes," which are geographical groups of five to 12 wards, similar to a diocese. The LDS Church has 3,004 stakes worldwide, 4 of which are based in Herriman. Stakes are presided over by a stake president, usually a married man who serves as an unpaid lay minster for approximately nine years. Stake members meet together in conferences twice a year for worship and instruction and also participate in service and social activities periodically throughout the year.

Since young, unmarried adults have spiritual and social needs that tend to differ from those of established families, young single adult wards are formed when there are 150 or more young single adults in a locale. Inclusion in these congregations is typically based on two criteria—age (18 to 30) and marital status (single). According to a Church handbook, "Membership in a young single adult ward is temporary. Leaders help young single adults prepare to return to a conventional ward when they marry or reach age 31." (Handbook) Membership in young single adult wards is voluntary. Young single adults can choose whether to attend the YSA ward for their area or the conventional ward for their area.

The LDS Church first established young adult congregations in 1968 as student wards in university settings. In 1976 the Church created young single adult wards to meet the needs of young adults who were not students. In 2011 the Church discontinued student wards and reorganized young single adult wards based on geographic boundaries irrespective of

student status. The Herriman YSA Ward was created as part of this reorganization. The Herriman YSA Ward is one of roughly 1,177 young single adult wards and branches the LDS Church sponsors, mostly in the western United States. "The focus of Church leaders is to make sure that all young single adults have a place to call home, with the opportunity to serve and have their own spiritual needs met."
(Mormon Newsroom)

As part of this 2011 reorganization, young single adult stakes were also created in areas with a high concentration of young single adults. The introduction of young single adult stakes allowed stake leaders to focus on the unique spiritual and social needs of young adults and to sponsor service and social activities more suited to the needs of these members. The Herriman YSA Ward is part of the Riverton YSA Stake. In areas with fewer LDS young single adults, a young single adult ward is often hosted by a conventional stake and may even be shared by shared by two neighboring conventional stakes. If there are not enough young single adults in an area for a congregation, a young single adult organization within the conventional ward or stake addresses the needs of these members.

Ward Meetings and Observations

The weekly Sunday services for the Herriman YSA Ward are three hours long and begin with a sacrament meeting at 1 p.m. followed by a Sunday School hour and concluding with an hour of instruction during which men attend priesthood meeting and women attend Relief Society meeting. They meet in a large, older, brown-brick building with arched windows and a black-and-white steeple on top. The front of the building has an etched-stone sign designating it as a meetinghouse for the Herriman Ward, Riverton Stake of The Church of Jesus Christ of Latter-day Saints. The building is surrounded by a large grass lawn, bushes, and large pine and shade trees.

The parking lot was filled on the Sunday of the research visit, and many had to park on the street. In the building one finds programs and blank nametags on a table near the entrance to the chapel. The chapel is in the center-rear of the building, along with a gymnasium that is separated from the chapel by accordion doors that can be opened to accommodate larger crowds.

The chapel was already very full. A young adult woman was playing prelude music on the organ while other young adults were chatting with one another throughout the chapel. About 150 young adults were at the meeting when it began, and six to 10 came in later. There was a fairly equal mix of young adult men and women. The majority were Caucasian, but some individuals were also of various ethnicities. The women wore dresses or skirts and blouses, and most men were in suits or button-up shirts and ties.

The meeting began with a welcome by Bishop Bruce Saunders, the married leader of the ward. He greeted visitors and new members and encouraged all to stay after the meetings that day for a nacho bar and socializing. The congregation then joined in singing an opening hymn, accompanied by the young woman on the organ. The young adult man conducting the music was unsure of his actions, but smiled broadly and made funny eyes at a friend in the audience as he did his best to move his arm in time with the music. He was a manifestation of the comfortable, informal atmosphere of the service. After an opening prayer offered by a young adult member of the ward, Bishop Saunders returned to the pulpit and read the names of new members who had recently moved into the ward. He had them stand—four young adult men and six young adult women—so the other members of the ward could greet them. He struggled to pronounce one of the names and laughed with the congregation and apologized to the young woman when he couldn't quite get it right. He then announced the names of men and women who had been called to serve on different committees in the ward and asked for a sustaining vote from ward members. He was very comfortable and friendly in his interactions with the ward members.

After the business of the ward was concluded, the congregation sang another traditional hymn while three young men prepared the emblems of the sacrament (bread and water), which were then passed to the members of the congregation by several other young men. This part of the service took about 15 minutes and was accompanied by a general spirit of reverence. I noticed a few members engaged with electronic devices, others reading from hymnbooks, and some sitting with their eyes closed in silent prayer or contemplation.

Following the sacrament, the bishop's wife, Holly, addressed the congregation. She asked questions, joked, and laughed with the congregants. Her remarks emphasized all the different relationships in their lives and the need to work at those relationships, sacrifice for those they love, and understand the give-and-take necessary for relationships to prosper. She gave many humorous examples from her own 20 years of marriage and family life and encouraged the members to seek out relationships that make them want to be better people. She also spoke of having a personal relationship with God and of challenging times in her own life when she wondered where her testimony of God had gone. She explained the roles of faith, hope, prayer, and trust in helping her face her own questions. She closed her remarks by expressing how much she and her husband loved being involved with the young adults.

Mrs. Saunders' remarks were followed by another hymn, and then Bishop Saunders addressed the congregation for the remainder of the meeting. He told his personal story of being diagnosed with cancer shortly after having their first child and buying their first home. He shared the process he went through of seeking after God and finding greater faith in his life, asking all to reflect on how they handle life's challenges. He encouraged all to "prepare for the storms, but live in the sunshine. Love the day you are in." He counseled the members to recognize the hand of God in their lives, to "get up and do," and to figure out what God's plan is for them. He admonished them to avoid drinking, pornography, and premarital sex, saying, "Don't view and do as the world does! If you want to win the race, run it God's way!"

At the conclusion of his remarks, Bishop Saunders invited those attending for the first time to come to a new member meeting and reminded all members about the game night the following evening. The meeting concluded with another congregational hymn and a closing prayer offered by a ward member. It is important to note that this was an atypical sacrament meeting. Though the flow of the meeting is usually the same, speakers for the program are usually members of the congregation selected in advance by the bishop or one of his two counselors.

The Bishop

Following the service, most ward members exited the chapel to attend other meetings. I introduced myself to the bishop and his wife. Holly Saunders is 44 years old, and she and Bishop Bruce Saunders, a 47-year-old general contractor, have been married 20 years and have four children. Mrs. Saunders explained that he bishop had served with the young adults in different capacities for about two and a half years, being called to serve as bishop of this ward six months earlier. She expressed how much she loves attending the ward and being with the young adults there, especially how beautiful it is to hear them sing. As the chapel cleared, the bishop kissed his wife and told her goodbye. We then sat on some pews in the back of the chapel and he told me about his service with the young adults.

He explained that his purpose is not to push dating and marriage, as may be the case in other young single adult wards. He said that though the Church promotes marriage and family, that step will happen when it happens. These men and women face many challenges and he wants them to be spiritually prepared to face those things. He said the ward has lots of activities and social events planned, but that he just supports those things because it is a part of the program. What is most important to him is the spiritual dimension to the work he does.

In response to a question about the challenges the members of his ward face, Saunders said he counsels with many that struggle with addictions, particularly pornography, and involvement in premarital sex. He says that discouragement often leads to those things. He explained that he attends a weekly 12-step addiction recovery program to help him be better able to counsel the men and women who come to him for help. Helping members with these issues is fundamental because living according to the Church's moral standard is a fundamental condition to receive a temple recommend (authorization from a bishop and stake leader) for attending the temple where active adult members participate in sacred ordinances, make personal covenants with God, and are sealed (united eternally) as families.

The bishop also said that the hardest appointments he has are with young women who express that they are living according to the principles they have been taught and done all they were asked to do and yet the marriage and family they so desperately want has not yet been a choice for them. This concern manifests the centrality of the theological belief in the importance of marriage and the eternal nature of family relationships. He expresses feelings of inadequacy when it comes to counseling these discouraged souls and confesses to praying in these moments that he will know what to say because, "They are Thy daughters first Lord, and there is no easy answer to that question."

Bishop Saunders said he sometimes spends four or five nights a week in various ward and stake meetings, visits, and interviews or counseling appointments with ward members. His stake leader says he should do less and only give two nights in addition to Sunday meetings, but sometimes the need is greater and he feels he can't turn people away. He said it's a hard balance because many ward members who come for appointments are really struggling. While helping in that way is important, he also wants to have time to reach out to those who are actively participating and not struggling. He said he generally doesn't do personal interviews during Church classes so he can instead attend them and interact with the ward members there. He also goes out one night a week with Mrs. Saunders to visit young adults in their homes.

When asked about the new member meeting, he explained that it is held after sacrament meeting each week in an effort to get to know the new men and women attending the ward. A member of the bishopric (usually one of the bishop's two counselors) attends that meeting and has a two-minute informal interview with each new member to get to know where they are from, how long they plan on attending the ward, and what their six-month goals are. This helps the leadership keep a handle on the changing membership of the ward. He says they currently have 327 members (167 men, 160 women) on record—meaning people who have been baptized as LDS Church members, who live in the ward boundaries, and who have attended the ward before. For the past two years they have had an average of 50 percent attendance at Sunday meetings. He tells me that attendance really depends on school schedules and a variety of other factors, but generally there are 160 to 180 in attendance. Today was a smaller group. Often an overflow area is opened behind the chapel to provide additional seating. Yet even in busy times, many members are unaccounted for. Some of the members on record may have moved away, some attend school other places and only come back occasionally, and some simply choose not to come. Ward missionaries (22 young adults and the bishop's wife) help keep track of these people, but the transient nature of this stage of life is a challenge for leaders.

While we were talking, a young woman walked by the chapel doors. Bishop Saunders called to her by name and asked about her younger sister, a member of the ward who was leaving that week to serve a Church mission for 18 months in Japan. He told her that he would come by their home that evening after his meetings to say goodbye. He later explained that in the six months since he has been bishop, 10 young adults have received a full-time missionary "call" (a specific assignment issued by the Church after an individual expresses interest to serve and submits required paperwork) to serve full-time missions. Full-time missionaries are different than ward missionaries. While ward missionaries continue with their regular work or schooling and serve in their ward area, full-time missionaries leave their families, friends, work, and school responsibilities and serve full-time in assigned areas throughout the world. Young adult men can serve any time after age 18 and serve for 24 months. Young adult women can serve any time after age 19 and serve for 18 months. Roughly 114 members of the ward have already completed full-time missions, which illustrates that this type of service is often central to the religious experience of young adults in this ward.

I asked Bishop Saunders what meetings and activities he would recommend I attend to get a feel for the ward, and he said the one thing I shouldn't miss is a monthly testimony meeting (a sacrament meeting in which spontaneous testimony is shared rather than having assigned speakers). He said the energy and testimony of the ward members and the experiences they share are powerful. He said and that the meeting always goes past the scheduled allotment of time. Outside of the regular Sunday meetings, activities greatly vary in type and attendance.

Bishop Saunders seems to be a genuine man who knows the men and women in his ward personally and cares deeply for them and their spiritual welfare. He willingly sacrifices a great deal of time for those he shepherds, especially considering this is a volunteer position and he also has a family and professional career to balance.

Stake Meetings and Observations

The Herriman YSA Ward is part of the Riverton YSA Stake. The stake is composed of 11 YSA wards—10 based on geographic regions and one Tongan ward whose members elect to attend that ward. The stake is housed in the Riverton YSA Stake Center in the Jordan Institute Building and seven other meetinghouses in the surrounding areas.

The stake holds a stake conference twice a year for all members of the 11 wards to attend worship services together. I attended one of these meetings. It was a two-hour meeting held at 1:00 p.m. on a Sunday in place of regular ward meetings. The conference included a service held the previous evening to provide additional inspiration and instruction. Upon entering the building that Sunday I was greeted by an older man in a suit and given a flyer about an upcoming "Young Single Adult Summit." The meeting was held in a chapel that opened into a gymnasium to accommodate the large crowd. Rows of chairs filled the gymnasium and a stage at the far end. Common areas with couches were also filled with young adults who listened to the meeting as it was broadcast throughout the building. Approximately 950-1000 young adults were in attendance. Most young men were dressed conservatively in suits or collared shirts and ties and young women wore skirts or dresses. However there were also a wide assortment of personal styles of dress as well as a variety of facial hair, Mohawks, and tattoos.

On the stand were the stake president, his two counselors, and their wives. Each of the men wore a handmade lei provided by members of the Tongan ward. The two-hour meeting, held in English, began with the congregation singing a traditional hymn followed by an opening prayer given by a young adult. The subsequent program included seven speakers. The first speaker was a dynamic 27-year-old young woman from the Herriman YSA ward. Using a very informal tone and eliciting laughter from the crowd, she spoke of her life journey and her deepening understanding of hope. She quoted Church leaders and scriptural stories to illustrate that for her, hope is like glow-in-the-dark stars that they all can hold on to in dark times. The next two speakers were the wives of two members of the stake presidency, who both expressed love for the young adults and gratitude for the opportunity to interact with them. One asserted, "You are a light to the world and to me!" and encouraged them to never give up on their hopes and dreams and to never forget Jesus Christ. The second woman referenced a recent movie, *Oz the Great and Powerful,* and the message that "you are greater than you know." She spoke highly of motherhood and of not running and hiding from challenges but aligning your life with God's will for you. The next speaker, who spoke of Christ as a light in dark times, was followed by a chorus of about 30 young adult men singing an LDS hymn, "Ye Elders of Israel."

Each of the three members of the stake presidency then addressed the group. The first speaker, one of the counselors, spoke candidly of the recent suicide of his nephew and the reality of the many challenges that members of the congregation face. He spoke of having strength, courage, and faith during these challenges and ended with a tender expression of love for the members of the stake. The other counselor began his remarks by showing a video of the personal stories of individuals and families from central Salt Lake City who the stake would be helping with home and yard improvements at an upcoming service project. After the video he spoke of acting in a temporal way just as Jesus Christ would and how to help build Zion. He encouraged the congregation to reach out and serve with greater charity, reminding them that "the pathway to happiness travels through other people." The concluding speaker was the stake president, who spoke of the robust spiritual world and the need for a personal anchor and connection with heaven. He taught the young adults to be vertically aligned with God's will for them and not horizontally aligned with the opinions and values of the world or the culture in which they live. He shared a number of testimonies written for him by young adult men and women in the stake about the scriptures and their power to connect a person with God. He issued a challenge to each member of the stake to read the entire Book of Mormon before they met for the next stake conference in six months. He encouraged them to read it, test it, and seek a personal witness that it is true. He invited them to share their experiences with the leadership and closed by saying, "God loves you—as do we."

After the meeting the young adults helped put away all of the chairs in the gymnasium area. Many mingled and laughed together in the meeting area and in the halls. As members left they were given reading schedules as a reminder of the challenge issued by the stake president.

Second Ward Meeting Observation

As suggested by the bishop, I later attended a "fast Sunday" meeting with the Herriman YSA Ward. On the first Sunday of each month, LDS Church members are invited to abstain from food and water for two meals as an act of spiritual discipline. They are also asked to donate the cost of those meals as a charitable contribution to help those in need. Sacrament meetings on these fast Sundays are unique in that speakers are not scheduled in advance; instead, anyone who would like to share his or her testimony is invited to do so. When I arrived I immediately noticed that something was different. This time, roughly 180 ward members were present when the meeting began. The back of the chapel was opened into the overflow area.

The first part of the meeting, conducted this time by one of the bishop's counselors, was very similar to the previous meeting. He announced a devotional meeting and choir practice being held that evening and a "get to know you bingo" activity the following evening. He encouraged the members to check the ward Facebook page for details about the activities. The meeting proceeded with a congregational hymn, an opening prayer, another congregational hymn, and the administration of the sacrament to members. At that point the man conducting the meeting returned to the pulpit and shared brief remarks about the scriptures and the challenge from stake leaders to read the Book of Mormon. He encouraged the congregants to read the scriptures prayerfully and shared his testimony that they would get answers to their personal questions—that God would speak to them. He then invited all who would like to share their testimonies to do so.

A handful of ward members walked to the stand immediately and shared their feelings and experiences one at a time in an "open mic" setting. The first was a man who shared that "if you put God first, everything will work out." A woman then shared some experiences from her first year as a schoolteacher and her feelings of falling short. She had attended the temple that week (LDS temples are holy places of worship where individuals make sacred promises with God and are separate from regular meetinghouses used for Sunday services; BYU). While she was there, she felt the impression that what she was doing was right and that God loved her. The next woman shared her feelings about a close friend with brain cancer and asked others to pray for him. She said that she feels like the scriptures are "juicy and delicious" and she loves what they bring to her life. She admitted that even though she had served a mission and taught other people about Jesus Christ, she still wants to learn to access His Atonement more in her life.   Another woman shared her experiences with reading from the Bible on her lunch break at work and how God spoke to her through a passage she read in Philippians. Another man explained that he was celebrating his one-year anniversary of coming back to the Church after spending a while on some undesirable paths. He shared that he was grateful for his "second chance with the Church" and testified of Jesus Christ and how he was able to "use the Atonement in a real way."

Over the course of the 75-minute meeting, seven women and five men shared their testimonies. As a researcher, it was valuable to observe these young adults in a natural setting as they shared with one another the personal experiences and struggles they are having and how their religion influences and guides their lives. While research has shown that adolescents and young adults are often "remarkably inarticulate" about their faith, I found these young adults to be remarkably articulate and candid about their faith in God and the salience of their religious beliefs in their everyday lives. Perhaps traditions such as this testimony meeting give LDS young adults the opportunity to practice talking about faith and the opportunity to see expressions of faith modeled by their peers. (Smith 2005)

A Variety of Activities

There are an amazing number of different, optional activities offered at the Herriman YSA Ward. The printed program from one meeting reminded ward members of the following activities scheduled for the next three weeks: (1) Mix & mingle—a light meal and opportunity to socialize held after church once a month. (2) Home evening—a weekly social gathering held at the meetinghouse every Monday evening. Activities might consist of get-to-know-you bingo, game nights, talent shows, etc. One evening a month is devoted to a community service project. Recent service projects included helping at an animal shelter, raking leaves, working at the food bank, raising money for a boy in the community with cancer, and shoveling snow. (3) Ward temple night—a monthly opportunity to attend a nearby LDS temple and then go out to eat with other ward members. (4) Stake temple night held twice a year in conjunction with stake conference. All members of the stake are invited to attend the temple and have dinner together afterward. (5) Institute classes; religious instruction classes held one night a week at a local building and also at the nearby community college. The program stated: "Be sure to register and attend institute. Depending on how many people we can get to register and attend institute, we will either throw pies at the bishopric's faces or wax their legs!" (6) Choir practice every Sunday evening for anyone who wants to participate. (7) Addiction recovery meetings; five different groups offered Sunday and Friday nights for young adults who need support in facing addictions in their own lives or the lives of loved ones. (8) Stake service project, a large project for all stake members aimed at home and yard renovations for needy residents of a nearby community. (9) Family history; Spanish speakers were asked to volunteer to help with a family history project and given a phone number to call for more details.

This list was not exhaustive. There was also an upcoming talent show for the stake as well as a two day "summit" for all the members of three young single adult stakes in the region (to include food, inspirational speakers, entertainment activities, and a luau). Certainly there are many opportunities for these young adults to engage spiritually and socially with other young adults in their ward, stake, and beyond. A young woman, 27-year-old Rebecca, said that in other young single adult wards she had sometimes attended activities only to support friends who were in charge of them. She has been in charge before and she knows what it is like, so she wants to support others who are in charge of activities now. Such relationship support, which is fostered by activities, seems to be an important dynamic among these congregants.

Expectation to Serve

The many activities are a manifestation of the leadership skills of the young single adult members of this ward. While some activities were planned in part by married adults, most of these activities were sponsored by committees of young adults who had accepted "callings" (requests from the bishopric to serve in a certain capacity) to staff them. One ward leader explained that there are 12 different committees that plan and lead different efforts: activities, employment/welfare, facilities, family history, music, technology, ward missionaries, temple, compassionate service, indexing (a part of family history), new member, and institute. In addition to these committees, young single adults make up the presidencies of the Sunday School,

Relief Society (women's group), and elders quorum (men's group), while other young single adults assist them, such as serving as teachers.

In addition to these leadership and teaching callings, most women in the ward are assigned as "visiting teachers" to visit other women in the ward in their homes monthly and share a gospel message (with slightly less than half of assigned visits being completed every month). Similarly, about half of the men in the ward are assigned as "home teachers," visiting men and women in the ward monthly and sharing a gospel message (with well over a third of the visits completed each month).

In a church where regular Sunday worship services are already three hours long, it may seem that asking for more time from young adults who already have busy lives would drive them away. Research shows the opposite to be true. Religious groups who expect more of their adherents tend to have members who are more committed to their religion and who exhibit more positive social outcomes. (Smith 2005) In the third wave (2008) of the National Study of Youth and Religion, which examines the religious and spiritual lives of 18 to 23-year-olds in the United States, researchers found that young adults who maintain that religion is important in their personal life are those who also demonstrate external expressions of faith, such as religious service attendance. Similarly, young adults who become less involved in external religious activities substantially reduce the internal importance of religion in their lives. (Smith 2009) Thus, these meetings and activities may provide a meaningful way to strengthen both the internal and external religious identity of ward members.

Drawing in the Next Cohort

As with most congregations of this age group, membership fluctuates and changes over time. Members marry and then attend conventional family wards, graduate from school and move away to begin careers, or in some cases, "age out" of the ward. Members age 31 and older are asked to attend conventional wards or, if available, a single adult ward for those age 31–45. With these events comes the awareness that maintaining the vitality of the ward requires drawing in the next cohort of young single adults. Samantha, the president of the Relief Society women's group, said that she had recently helped with a devotional meeting for graduating high school seniors in a local conventional stake to learn about young single adult wards. This meeting included young adult speakers who described the different types of activities the ward sponsors and details about the institute program and the classes available. The event also featured a musical number by the young single adult men's choir. Samantha said, "It was really fun because with the choir members there you really could see how we have a lot of fun in the YSA ward and we also come to be spiritually fed and not just get married, get married, get married." She explained that the purpose of the meeting was not to recruit new members but to make them aware that the young single adult ward is there and that they are welcome at it. Samantha lamented, "Sadly, this [meeting] consisted of only 12 youth, but I still think it was a success because a lot of the shepherding couples (older adults asked to serve young single adults in conventional wards) came and got a good glimpse into what goes on at the young single adult ward and can therefore better communicate that to young single adults in the conventional wards."

A Variety of Ward Members

Perhaps the best illustration of spiritual and social life in this congregation is a cross-section of some of the individuals met while conducting this research. Names have been changed.

(1) Alex is a mixed race, African American/Caucasian young man, mid-20s, with mid-length dark hair and partial beard. He was wearing black pants, a black shirt, and chains around his neck. Mrs. Saunders told him that she had missed him at meetings lately. He explained that he had been playing

Sunday poker instead, and that he had taken third and won $50 the week before. She playfully asked which was better, $50 or "having the Spirit" in his life. They talked for a few minutes and then the bishop put a hand on Alex's shoulder and said that Alex may look rough on the outside, but those who hear Alex share his testimony know he has a soft heart on the inside. Alex described himself as a "combat fighter" who had been involved in gangs and other things in a different city but didn't want to participate anymore because he saw too many of his friends get killed. He agreed that he does have a soft heart inside but that it is pretty bruised. He said he's not really sure what he believes and still has a lot of questions. He mentioned a conversation he had with his brother about religion and politics. While his brother has more Protestant beliefs, Alex is still trying to figure out what he believes and wants to do with his life.

(2) *Lindsay and Kathy*: At the first meeting, there was a library/materials center where two young women were talking and laughing after the meeting. They said they were best friends and had been attending the ward for about year and a half. They had attended the same conventional ward when they were younger. They started attending this ward the fall after they graduated from high school.

Lindsay is a slender 20-year-old with long brown hair. She wore a sticker nametag on her dress that read, "My name is ... **awesome**." When asked what she liked about the ward, Lindsay said that in the family ward she felt she was seen as a child and not really an individual. She is glad to now have a calling and be involved in the ward and said she feels a sense of unity and connectedness here. She said that she really likes the fact that dating isn't a huge part of the ward culture and that both the current bishop and the bishop before him are "awesome" and really seem to care about her as a person. She said that she always attends the institute classes during the week. She doesn't always remember which scriptures they talked about, but she remembers the discussions about how they apply to her life. She really likes the discussions.

Kathy is a short 19-year-old who wore a flower circlet in her long blonde hair. She was animated as she concurred with Lindsay that the bishop really cares about them and is very sensitive. She said that she likes how it doesn't matter what age people are because everyone is friendly with everyone else in the ward. She told about a recent ward talent show. She sang part of the song "God Help the Outcasts" from Les Miserable that she sang for the show. Kathy said she doesn't attend the same institute class as Lindsay. She is involved on the institute council (a young adult leadership group) and attends institute at a nearby community college during the week. She talked about how much she likes the social connection and the relationships there.

(3) Bridger is a dynamic, athletically built, blond 22-year-old who is currently a college student. Bridger is the only member of the Church in his family. Though he sometimes has conflicts with his parents (particularly his dad) about the time he spends at church activities, he said it is worth it because it is so important to him. He told me that he regularly attends meetings and activities because he loves "to go get spiritual with a bunch of friends." Bridger served a two-year mission for the LDS Church and returned about a year ago. He briefly attended a conventional ward after his mission but said that "got old" really fast and he wanted to be with other young adults. He said he had been engaged to be married, and when things didn't work out he had a hard time. He shared that he has commitment issues now when it comes to dating girls but that he feels very comfortable with his friends. He said: "We're in it together. We're in the same situation, and it's fun." Bridger serves as a ward missionary. He explained that there are about nine young adults serving as ward missionaries. They visit ward members who don't regularly come to church. They reach out to them, invite them to activities, and try to be friends with them. Bridger admits that he loves to go to activities and "make people feel awkward" because he thinks (laughingly) it is a great way to get people out of their comfort

zone and open them up. He laughed and said that's the best way to get to know people.

(4) Jenna was a speaker at stake conference. She is a very animated 27-year-old bank teller who has attended the Herriman YSA Ward for about two years. She said she "ward-hopped" for a number of years until the Church reorganized the wards and designated wards based on geographic locations. At first she didn't like the ward because she didn't know people, but she then made a goal to attend every activity the ward sponsored. She said it is a challenge to balance friends, her calling as a ward missionary, her job, and her boyfriend, but she feels that participating in the many activities has been really good for her and helped her get to know people and feel included. Jenna says the bishop has occasionally asked her to reach out to specific people and be their friend because he knows they are struggling. She really feels connected with the bishop, who she told me often texts her words of encouragement and even attended a volleyball game of the team she plays on with other ward members. When asked about her life goals for the next five years, Jenna joked that "plan A" includes getting married (possibly to her boyfriend who she met in the ward), starting a family, and serving in the Church as a Young Women leader (serving in the organization for girls age 12–17). "Plan B" includes advancing her position at work and attending either a ward for older singles or a conventional ward. When asked how being in the young single adult ward helps with her life goals she answered that it helps her to not become stagnant in who she is; interacting with many different young adults and seeing the different paths they are taking helps her reevaluate her life and choices and helps her become who she wants to be.

(5) Jared came up to a woman being interviewed during the Sunday School hour and in a cheerful but authoritative tone told her that she needed to be in class, to which she playfully responded that he needed to get to class too. She gave him a big hug and told him that she needed to talk to me for a few minutes but she would go to class later. Jared has Down

syndrome, and though he is older than 31, ward leaders support his continued membership in the ward because of his unique circumstances. It was clear that Jared is a valued member of the ward. At a recent ward talent show, Jared performed an act as a "super hero." He demonstrated, with "great sound effects," how he could lift the audience and throw them around the gymnasium using simple arm movements, and ward members played along by moving their bodies in response to his movements. Jared was disappointed that he didn't win first place but was satisfied with the "Most Original" award. The men in the ward coordinate weekly efforts to provide rides for Jared to and from ward activities.

(6) Valerie is a 26-year-old business executive with immaculately styled hair and professionally manicured nails. She had been attending the ward for about five months and described this as "a new chapter" in her life. She candidly shared that a few years ago she was engaged, and when the relationship abruptly ended it caused her faith and her identity to be shaken. She turned away from the Church and got involved with a new crowd of friends, resulting in doing things that she had previously believed were wrong. She graduated from college and had great success in her business career, but she felt unhappy and was "not headed where [she] wanted to be." She said that even though she didn't want to go to church at the time, she still knew that God was there and cared about her. She said she prayed intently that God would help her know where to go and what to do so she could change her life and find happiness. She described a rapid sequence of events that landed her "the perfect job" and prompted her to move to Utah.
She affirmed that it was God opening the doors for her. Right after moving here, Valerie met with Bishop Saunders and began attending the Herriman YSA Ward to help reestablish her spiritual and religious roots. She vividly described her "spiritual backpack" and how bad choices she had made in the past were like rocks she was carrying around. She said that counseling with the bishop has helped her remove the unnecessary baggage so she has room for the things that are

important in her life. She explained that for the past few years she has had very little contact with her parents but that her mom is visiting soon. Valerie is hopeful about reestablishing a relationship with her. She showed a small heart-shaped tattoo on her ankle and said it is a symbol of her journey. Though the LDS Church discourages members from getting tattoos, she said it is the perfect symbol of her nontraditional path to come to know herself and have God and spirituality be a part of her life, and she never wants to forget that. Valerie said that she doesn't participate in many of the ward's activities outside of Sunday meetings because she often works 70 hours a week, but she does play in a volleyball league at the community recreation center with a team of friends from the ward.

The Herriman YSA Ward is a melting pot for a wide variety of young adults. I spoke with young adults of all ages—students, teachers, business professionals; some living at home, some on their own in the world; some deeply rooted spiritually and some were searching for faith. The one thing they had in common was that they call this congregation home. The different stories of the individuals lends valuable perspective about what the ward has to offer these young adults and why they make this faith community a part of their lives.

Finances

As with all LDS wards, funding for the Herriman YSA Ward is allocated from the LDS Church. These funds come from the general members of the LDS Church, who are asked to pay 10% of their income as tithing, as well as other voluntary contributions to support Church initiatives. The paying of tithing is an expression of religious devotion in various religious traditions since ancient times. While specific numbers are unavailable, a large number of active young adult ward members regularly contribute a tithe as an expression of their religious commitment.

Tithing is used to fund Church operations in general and is also allocated back to individual wards and budgeted for use by different ward organizations. The LDS Church has a lay ministry, so Church funds are not used to support local leaders. Specific details regarding the budget of the Herriman YSA Ward were unavailable.

Key Dynamics

The original question of this paper is, what is it that draws young adults to participate in this congregation? Based on observations and interviews, this researcher believe this congregation demonstrates five key dynamics that form a foundation for this faith community: meaningful relationships, adult and peer role models, a robust social environment, opportunities for larger service, and theological and pragmatic tools to help young adults face life challenges.

First and foremost, every young adult interviewed mentioned or demonstrated how relationships are a key factor in their involvement in the young single adult ward. The relationships with married adult leaders were very important, and Bishop Bruce Saunders is a stellar example of a personable leader who is invested in the lives of the young adults he shepherds. His visits in their homes and involvement at their activities foster meaningful personal relationships. That is no small feat in a congregation this size. In addition, counseling with him individually has had a life-changing impact on many young adults.

The relationships formed with peers are also fundamental. Having people who know you and love you is important to most people. It is clear that the leaders of this ward recognize that and encourage members to reach out in friendship both in the context of Church activities (such as the efforts of the missionary committee) and in other activities (such as the community volleyball team). Many individuals expressed that they felt acceptance from the other young adults and that they didn't have to change who they were in order to fit in to the ward. The young adults were very open and honest with the interviewer and in their testimonies to each other about the challenges they have faced and the choices they have made in their lives. The initial observation of the young man conducting the music in sacrament meeting attested to the fact that perfection is not required to be a part of this congregation—trying hard is good enough. Genuine interpersonal connections are valuable, and this faith community and its members seem to foster authentic relationships.

The second dynamic, tied closely with the first, is the presence of married adult and peer mentors. Mentoring in this context provides examples of successful marriage and family life, facing challenges with faith, and living a Christian life of commitment and sacrifice. At the first meeting and stake conference attended for research, the male leaders of the ward and stake sat next to their wives on the stand, and both husbands and wives were involved in the instruction given to the congregation. They shared serious and humorous stories of struggles and triumphs in their marriages and families. One may observe an affectionate connection between the bishop and his wife as they interact with ward members. In a church where marriage and family are foundational, it seems relevant to have examples of individuals who demonstrate joy found in traditional marriage and family roles. (Gay members are welcome, but they are expected to live celibate lives, as are straight single members.) Examples of strong family relations seem particularly important because many young adults aspire to have their own families but may not come from positive family situations. In addition, the sermons and testimonies shared by adults and peers at the meeting gave specific examples of facing life challenges—from job loss to cancer and addictions to suicide—with faith and hope. The bishop and other older and younger leaders are also remarkable examples of what it means to sacrifice in order to live a Christian life. As Jenna asserted, the lives of other young adults in her ward helped her reevaluate her own life and move forward in her goals.

A third dynamic that seems to attract young adults to this congregation is the robust social environment. Activities are planned for nearly every night of the week, constantly providing young adults with a place to be and something to do that is in harmony with the standards of the LDS Church. Activities such as game nights, talent shows, softball games, and dinners provide opportunities for ward members to get to know one another and have fun together in a non-religious setting. At the same time, midweek religious instruction and temple activities provide times for the men and women to practice their religion within a social context and, as Bridger said, "get spiritual with a bunch of friends." The structure of ward and stake groups provides both a smaller and larger context for these young adults to socialize and get to know other young adults who share their beliefs and standards. Many hope that such social opportunities will eventually lead to a happy marriage within the faith.

The fourth dynamic observed as a significant factor in young adult involvement in this ward was opportunities for larger service. In his research of young adults in the United States, Christian Smith and his colleagues found that one of the great challenges facing young adults is a disengagement from civic life. (Smith 2011) Traditions in the wider culture can make life more about ease and pleasure and less about being connected to the lives and needs of others. This faith community challenges that norm by inviting young adults to be a part of something bigger than themselves through meaningful service. That service sometimes takes place in small groups as part of home evening (Monday night) activities each month when ward members partner with individuals and agencies in the community (such as the food bank and animal shelter). It may also take place in a larger group, such as with the stake service activity to help renovate homes and yards of families in need. (Deseret News) Another profound example of larger service is devoting 18 to 24 months as a missionary for the Church, which many of the young adults in this ward had done or were preparing to do. Most active members serve in callings or accept assignments.

Clearly, this faith community helps provide members with opportunities for larger service.

The fifth key dynamic observed in this faith community is the presence of theological and pragmatic tools to help young adults face life challenges. Researcher Kenda Dean states, "Cultural tools are the symbols, stories, rituals, relationships and worldviews that we pick up from our experience of the world around us . . . and we use them to construct meaning and guide our actions in the world." (Dean 2010) Some of the tools I observed include clear teachings and moral directives based on LDS theology, leadership opportunities, coping skills, addiction recovery support, personal counseling with trusted leaders, spiritual experiences, and relationship networks. Young adulthood is filled with questions, difficulties, and transitions that often challenge in dramatic ways the identity formation process of individuals. The tools these young men and women are exposed to through active participation in this faith community provide them valuable resources for weathering life's storms and establishing clear personal identities. However, the presence of these tools does not guarantee that all young adults will choose to use them. Society and prior life experiences offer other tools that often compete with or sabotage the tools offered in the context of the faith community. While that is to be expected, the faith community gives the young adults many positive tools that can be employed to cope with challenges and develop a mature identity.

One tool of particular interest is the strong influence of moral directives. Members are admonished repeatedly to avoid drug and alcohol use, pornography, and premarital sexual activity. Some of these standards may seem counter-cultural today. However, Smith and colleagues explain that their research shows three other major life challenges facing young adults today are confused moral reasoning, routine intoxication, and regrettable sexual experiences. (Smith 2011) These behaviors lead to troubled, unstable identities and troubles with engaging fully in an adult world. The presence of strong moral directives in this young single adult ward potentially insulates young adults from the negative consequences associated with these behaviors. Once again, being taught these standards does not mean the young adults always choose to follow them, but they are given access to teachings and mentors that exemplify why the standards are important even when they are not popular.

These five key dynamics contribute to the vibrant spiritual and social environment in the Herriman YSA Ward. While every member does not experience these elements in the same way, they help create a gathering place for young adults to return to again and again as a home for their souls.

Challenges in the Young Single Adult Ward

While the Herriman YSA Ward enjoys a core of active members, it must be said that some young adults only participate occasionally; some prefer to attend a conventional ward instead; and some have become "lost" and don't attend LDS services anywhere. In seeking to understand why people do attend, we must also reflect on why they do not. One interviewee was Adrienne, an alert, short-haired, 26-year-old phlebotomist who attended the Herriman YSA Ward for nine months after she returned from a mission to Canada. About nine months ago she decided to attend a conventional ward with her family instead of the Herriman YSA Ward because she felt the people there were too young and she "just didn't mesh." Someone in the ward had also asked about her about not being married yet and she didn't like that. She said she may attend a young single adult ward when she moves away from home, but for now Adrienne is a reminder that every young adult experiences the young single adult social setting and relationships differently, and those experiences influence if and where they choose to continue worshiping. Her experience brings up two challenges in the young single adult wards—age diversity and outlook on marriage.

First, these LDS congregations serve young adults ages 18 to 30. This is a large age range and encompasses individuals with different maturity levels and life experiences. It is during this time that young adults experience many transitions toward independence, including moving away from home, attending college, beginning careers, becoming financially independent, and experimenting with different beliefs and relationships. This naturally creates a very diverse congregation. In the Herriman YSA Ward, 238 members are 18 to 24 years old, and 103 are 25 years old or older. While this diversity provides mentorship for younger members, older members may come to feel that they don't belong, as Adrienne expressed. When discussing the challenges of ministering to a diverse ward, Samantha, the 27-year-old president of the Relief Society, said, "Those people who are done with school and working in their professional lives have very different interests than the recent high school graduates and the newly returned missionaries." She said they tried doing women's activities for members over 25, but they were asked to discontinue them because of the division it created among the ward members. Samantha expressed: "Some of the older sisters were really disappointed because they felt like they were finally finding people their age to go do fun things with. It's just a challenge since a lot of the guys who are in the 25-plus age range are not active or, if they are, they don't actively participate in the activities and are good at staying under the radar. So it is just hard."

Second, these young adults belong to a faith that believes strongly in the importance of marriage and family. Their presence in a young *single* adult ward highlights that they are single. As Bishop Saunders indicated, many ward members, particularly women, struggle with that and long for the opportunity to be married. To put the marriage issue into perspective, the median age at first marriage in the United States is 28.0 for men and 26.2 for women, while the median age at first marriage in Utah is 26.1 for men and 23.5 for women—the lowest in the nation. (Utah Jobs) This is largely due to the high concentration of LDS members in the population. This cultural expectation to marry and the resultant frustration for those who may remain unmarried, whether by choice or lack of opportunity, may lead some to migrate to a more secular community where marriage isn't seen as the expected trajectory for young adults. At the same time, many men and women find camaraderie with other single members and like that aspect of the ward. Samantha explained, "Sometimes I think a lot of sisters feel like they must have something wrong with them and that is why they are not married. In the singles ward, I have met so many amazing sisters! And I think to myself.... *There is nothing wrong with them! They are fantastic women of God! This is just part of His plan for them.* When I think that about the other sisters in my ward, it helps me accept my singleness as part of His plan for me too. Sometimes in our "Mormon culture" it feels like you shouldn't be happy if you are single ... which is ridiculous! I think the singles ward has given me so many great examples of hope and faith and joy!"

Another challenge members of the young single adult ward may face is that while all members are currently single, some have been married before. These men and women may find themselves single again due to divorce or the death of a spouse. These life experiences create a unique set of challenges that other young adults may not understand.

There is no perfect arrangement to solve any of these challenges, and not all young adults will find a place where they feel at home with other congregants. This is likely the case with all faith communities. This LDS ward and others like it simply do their best to provide a spiritual and social environment where young single adults can connect, learn, serve, and worship together.

Best Practices

While some key dynamics are peculiar to the structure and theology of its LDS roots, the Herriman YSA Ward also employs some practices that contribute to the efficacy of its ministry to young adults. These practices are easily replicable by other young adult ministries. One such practice is actively involving the young adults in the leadership, planning, and teaching of the congregation. This level of involvement strengthens commitment and fosters a sense of ownership in the congregation.

Another practice at work in the Herriman YSA Ward is effective communication and social networking. The printed program one meeting contained announcements for upcoming events, phone numbers for married adult and young adult leaders in the ward, meeting schedules, and classroom locations within the building. It also contained directions for accessing information about the ward and stake in a variety of electronic formats, including a weekly email list for the ward and text reminders from the stake.

Facebook: The printed program invited members to join the ward Facebook group. The Facebook group has 263 members, who regularly update it. Recent posts were from teachers (*"It's that time again! I'm teaching this Sunday, Gospel Principles Lesson 18, Faith in Jesus Christ room 108 at 2:10 p.m. Please come and support me!"*), and activity coordinators (*"Softball games tonight at 7 and 8! Bring a glove or two if you have one and come play. Same place as last week."*). This Facebook page also has pictures of past activities and is a forum where members can ask questions (*"So is the Relationships Institute class just for married couples or is it just for anyone and what is it about? What time and day is it on?"*) and invite people to join in on other social activities not sponsored by the ward. (*"I'm thinking of going up to Fifth Water Hot Springs Saturday morning and coming down late afternoon-ish. It's an hour and a half drive and an hour hike up to the hot spring. Let me know if you want to go, anyone's invited"*). This social network site provides a way for the young adults to stay connected with one another and informed about ward activities.

The Riverton YSA Stake also has a Facebook page, with 701 group members. This forum provides similar opportunities for members of the stake to connect and seek help (*"I am looking for an apartment in South or West Jordan close to a bus route.*

Please message me if you know of anything."). Reminders are also posted for stake activities *("Come sing in the summit choir! We will be performing in the Tabernacle, an awesome opportunity! Rehearsal is Sunday.")* This type of networking is an important way to facilitate connections among young adults.

Video Invitation: After stake conference, the stake president explained about this research project and the young adults in his stake. He talked about a new way he found to connect with the stake members and send out reminders. He had recorded a brief video in which he spoke to the members, reminding them about the stake conference and associated activities and inviting them to participate. Another leader in the stake then sent the video out to stake members via cell phones or email. This was the first time this form of communication had been used, but the response was very positive and the leaders plan to use it again. When asked about the video invitation, one member of the Herriman YSA Ward replied, "I did see the video invitation from the stake president about stake conference. I thought it was cool. I thought it was a good way for people to put a name with a face. Most of the time people don't get to know the stake president very well. With so many people moving in and out it was nice. I think less-actives benefited from it as well. [The stake president's] sincerity and love really showed through."

In addition to these forms of communication, the stake sponsors a Twitter feed that leaders post on regularly to send messages and encouragement to stake members. Recent tweets include, *"We love you! —Stake Presidency"* and *"[The stake president] wants to personally thank everyone who came to Stake Conference & he looks forward to our Book of Mormon challenge."* This shows that leaders are using the resources of this digital age to connect with and minister to the sheep in their fold.

Conclusion

Danielle stated, "God reaches into every part of our lives." From observations of this congregation, this researcher also believes that membership in the Herriman YSA Ward reaches into every part of the lives of these young men and women. This religious group ministers to congregants in temporal and spiritual ways and provides a community of friends and mentors to support young adults in the many challenges inherent in this stage of life. This faith community expects a great deal from members, but most young people seem to take it in stride and gladly incorporate their religion, including commitments to serve and worship, into their busy lives.

While older leaders have a significant impact on the men and women in the ward, it did not seem that the efficacy of the program was dependent on the charisma or talent of the married leaders. This is largely due to the structure and policies established by the LDS Church to assist those who administer young single adult wards. Thus, the Herriman Young Single Adult Ward is not necessarily an "outstanding congregation" but is likely representative of what many LDS young single adult wards are like throughout the United States. The primary difference among these wards would be the size of the congregation (with larger, more compact wards near the center of the Church in Utah) and whether they are part of a conventional stake or a young single adult stake.

This congregation offers meaningful relationships, significant role models, engaging social events, far-reaching service opportunities, diverse tools and resources for facing life challenges, important leadership opportunities, and substantial theological teachings that provide meaning in the lives of the men and women who come to worship here. Membership in this young adult faith community is certainly more a way of life than a weekly Sunday activity.

Emily Layton, M.S., is a qualitative researcher who studies the influence of religion and spirituality in the lives of Jewish, Christian, and Muslim individuals and families. Her prior work has focused on religious commitment, religious exploration in adolescence, and identity formation. She is a wife and a mother of five children and enjoys serving in her local LDS congregation.

References

BYU, https://familylife.byu.edu/Dollahite/Dollahite/S-60%20The%20Mormon%20American%20Family%20chap%20ETHNIC%20FAMILIES%20IN%20AMERICA%202012.pdf

Dean, K. C. (2010). *Almost Christian: What the faith of our teenagers is telling the American church*. New York: Oxford University Press, p 48.

Deseret News, www.deseretnews.com/article/865580295/Hundreds-of-volunteers-tackle-service-projects-in-Salt-Lake-City.html?pg=all

General Conference Statistical Report, www.lds.org/general-conference/2013/04/statistical-report-2012?lang=eng

Handbook, www.lds.org/handbook/handbook-2-administering-the-church/single-members/16.2#162

Mormon Newsroom, www.mormonnewsroom.org/article/organizational-changes-young-single-adults

Smith, C. and Denton, M. L. (2005). *Soul searching: The religious and spiritual lives of American teenagers*. New York: Oxford University Press.

Smith, C. and Snell, P. (2009). *Souls in transition: The religious and spiritual lives of emerging adults*. New York: Oxford University Press, p 252.

Smith, C.; Christoffersen, K.; Davidson, H.; and Herzog, P. S. (2011). *Lost in transition: The dark side of emerging adulthood.* New York: Oxford University Press.

Utah, http://jobs.utah.gov/wi/pubs/womencareers/factsheet.html

Chapter 5
Houston Bahá'í Center

By Michael McMullen

Young adults in the Baha'i faith must deal with the challenge of how to serve humanity in a religion with no clergy. A visitor walking into the lobby of the Houston Bahá'í Center is immediately greeted by friendly faces and the invitation to look at the historical display about the Bahá'í Faith in a room off the lobby, or join worshipers in the basement for coffee/tea and breakfast before the main Sunday morning worship service. The historical display provides information about the origins of the Bahá'í Faith in mid-19th century Iran, as well as communicating the principles of the religion established by Baha'u'llah, the prophet-founder of the Bahá'í community in 1864: the equality of men and women, the unity of all humanity, and the development of world peace through global governance, resulting in the establishment of the Kingdom of God through Bahá'í teachings and administration.

When visitors descend to the basement in the old, converted office building in mid-town Houston, they come upon a coffee-house set up with pastries, fruit, Persian tea in a Samovar, and coffee on a table against the back wall. Some younger kids are playing table-tennis, while young and old sit chatting around small, round tables before the worship program. There are a mix of whites, blacks, Hispanics, Asians, and a significant number of Persians. There are many young adults in attendance, but also elderly Bahá'ís, some of whom are Persians refugees to the US tell and can tell stories about their escape from the attempted genocide committed by the Shiite Muslim authorities in Iran, or recount the ongoing persecutions of the Bahá'í minority in Iran.

At 10 am, everyone is invited to go upstairs to the main hall for the morning's devotional program, prepared by the young adult members of the Houston Bahá'í community. Sanjay, an Indian/Hindu convert to the Bahá'í Faith, welcomes everyone to the Bahá'í center as chair of the nine-member Local Spiritual Assembly, and Nabil, one of the Persian-American young adults, begins the recorded music.

In the Bahá'í Faith, there are no clergy since Baha'u'llah has forbidden them, so Sanjay's role is not as a clergy member, but comes from being on the Local Spiritual Assembly of the Houston Bahá'í community. Bahá'ís are counseled in their scripture to elect every year a nine-member assembly to govern the affairs of the local community; a similar process occurs at the National and International Levels of Bahá'í Administration.

The music of several young Bahá'í singers/composers is introduced via YouTube (for example, Luke Slott, Andy Grammar, Karim Rushdy or Nabil Moghaddam), but sometimes there is also live music by hip-hop or rock-inspired Bahá'í singers. Interspersed between the music are prayers read or chanted (in Farsi) by high school youth. After about 30-45 minutes of prayers and singing, Sanjay introduces the speaker for the morning.

The speaker at the Sunday morning devotionals is usually a knowledgeable Bahá'ís who gives a 45-minute lecture on Bahá'í history, spirituality, the importance for Bahá'ís to teach their faith and communicate the religion of Baha'u'llah to the masses who have not yet heard about Baha'u'llah being the return of Christ. Over half the weekly devotional speakers are young adults.

Children's Class Teachers

While the devotional is going on in the main floor assembly hall, upstairs, Bahá'í "Sunday School" is taking place. Children's classes for ages preschool through 12th grade are held in individual classrooms, nearly all of them taught by young adults. Bahá'ís strongly emphasize the education of children, and one way this manifests itself is for Bahá'í communities to provide children's classes.

At the younger level classes, ages 5-10, Bahá'í education focuses on learning the basics of Bahá'í history, who the "Central Figures" of the Bahá'í Faith are, and basics of Bahá'í spiritual values, such as the unity of religion, the oneness of God, and the unity of humanity and working to develop a world without racial, gender or national prejudice.

In Bahá'ís history, the Faith begins with Ali-Muhammad, a Persian merchant born in 1817 who fulfills Shiite prophesy as being the return of the 12th Imam. Bahá'í theology states that the role of the return of the 12th Imam is to herald the coming of a prophet of global religious significance, who Bahá'ís believe to be the prophet-founder of their Faith, Baha'u'llah. As such, Bahá'ís believe that because the one God is the author of all the world's major faith traditions revealed at different historical times, Baha'u'llah is not only the return of Christ, but also the promised one of Islam, the Messiah anticipated by the Jews, the reincarnation of Krishna, and the 5th avatar of Buddha. After Baha'u'llah's death in 1892, the Bahá'í Faith was led by 'Abdu'l-Baha, the son of Baha'u'llah, from 1892-1921, and then by Shoghi Effendi, the great-grandson of Baha'u'llah, from 1921-1957. Shortly after Shoghi Effendi's death, the Bahá'ís of the world elected their first nine-person Universal House of Justice (UHJ). Given that there are no clergy allowed in the Bahá'í Faith, the UHJ collectively is the highest authority in the Bahá'í world.

Higher grade levels learn more specifics about other religions such as Zoroastrianism, Hinduism, Buddhism, Judaism, Christianity and Islam, which Bahá'ís consider to be all part of the "progressive revelation" of Prophets from God. Bahá'í classes for children ages 12-15 also focus on learning the basics of Bahá'í Administration. Young adults teach kids about the basics of Bahá'í governance, elections, and the intricacies of both the elected and appointed positions of the Bahá'í structure.

For kids 16-18 years old, the young adult teachers focus on issues that most impact not only high school kids, but also young adult Bahá'ís. For example, Bahá'ís are not allowed to drink alcohol or take drugs, engage in sexual intercourse outside of marriage or engage in backbiting. Bahá'í young adults therefore lead their peers in tough discussions about how to live "the Bahá'í life" of chastity and no mind-altering substances. Bahá'í young adults, like the high school-age students they teach, are challenged to live up to the high standards of Bahá'í morality, especially prohibitions against alcohol and premarital sex. Thus, for young adult Bahá'ís, working as youth teachers serves two main functions: (1) planning lessons for the 100 or so Bahá'í children who come to Sunday Bahá'í School reinforces their identity as Bahá'í teachers, an important aspect of the Bahá'í Faith where teaching a relatively unknown religion takes on great spiritual significance and is given high status; and (2) it allows young adult Bahá'ís a chance to serve in a high-visibility role in a faith with no clergy.

Bahá'í young adults make up about 16.5 percent of the 600-person Houston Bahá'í community. However, they comprise only about 9 percent of Local Spiritual Assembly members, 28 percent of those attending regular "deepenings" (what in Bahá'í-language would be considered "Bible studies"), and 21 percent of the membership on local committees.

Junior Youth Mentors

Another role for young adults in the Bahá'í Faith is to act as mentors to Junior Youth. In the Bahá'í Faith, 11-14-year olds are considered junior youth, and 15-30-year-olds are youth. This cutoff is different than some other groups, because Bahá'í law considers 15 to be the age of consent for young people to officially join Bahá'í membership rolls. With no clergy, Bahá'í leadership is selected by election, and the age at which Bahá'ís can officially enroll and get a Bahá'í number to vote in Bahá'í elections, give to Bahá'í funds, is age 15.

This is also the age when they are required to follow the obligatory laws of prayer and fasting.

Nearly all junior youth leaders are young adults. Meetings with 11-14-year-olds are held in young adults' homes. There is a special curriculum that young adult leaders are required to complete in order to be junior youth mentors. This curriculum was developed by the Columbian Bahá'í community, and is now referred to as the Ruhi Course Sequence throughout the Bahá'í world. Junior youth meetings involve completing lessons from a junior youth curriculum developed by the National Spiritual Assembly of the US, learning about responsibilities of junior youth to teach their friends about the Bahá'í Faith, and then having a meal together. At the end of all of the lessons, young adults lead the junior youth in some type of service project, such as a beach clean-up, bagging food for distribution to needy seniors, or visiting a nursing home.

One young adult I interviewed who is deeply involved in the Training Institute process said, "The courses designed by the National Assembly are helping empower junior youth. It is helping them understand they should develop a life of service, not just to other Bahá'ís, but to all young people—in their neighborhoods and communities." He emphasized that given the deteriorating condition of society, he is pushing young Bahá'ís to think about how they can make a positive change in the world.

Another young adult woman I interviewed said that the National Spiritual Assembly of the US has given more focus in the last five years to supporting youth and enhancing their spiritual education. She said "the goal is not only to help them lead a life of service to humanity, but to also have the human resources to grow up to be members of the Local Spiritual Assemblies and to be Assistants to Auxiliary Board members." She went on to say that when one goes to a Unit Convention (part of the process to elect the National Spiritual Assembly), everyone in attendance is over 50 years old, and most LSA members are older too. However, the "youth are the ones who are empowered to serve Baha'u'llah and their fellow human beings, who will be the ones who effectively teach the Bahá'í message, and who will win the goals of the current 5-Year Plan."

Auxiliary Board members are an appointed branch of the Bahá'í Administrative Order that act as consultants to the LSAs and NSAs to spread the Bahá'í message. At the global level, the Universal House of Justice develops "Plans" for the growth and development of the Bahá'í world community that gets filtered down to the National Spiritual Assemblies and then to the local level. The Bahá'í world is currently carrying out their teaching work via the "5-Year Plan."

Messages from Bahá'í leaders about the importance of young adults being the role models for youth and junior youth can be seen in the following statement: "By instilling in the junior youth a keen sense of purpose, the programme has demonstrated a remarkable capacity to transform young people, increase their commitment to spiritual and material education, empower them to undertake social action for the improvement of their communities, resist the destructive and prejudicial forces within their societies, and contribute to the construction of a better world." ("Insights from the Frontiers of Learning," by the International Teaching Centre, Bahá'í World Center, Haifa, Israel. April 2013, p. 4.)

Conclusion

The above discussion highlights some of the important roles performed in the Houston Bahá'í community by young adult Bahá'ís. As can be seen, although Bahá'ís have no official clergy, there are leadership roles, and young adults serve as worship leaders, children's classes teachers, and as junior youth mentors.

Bahá'í young adults make up about 16.5 percent of the 600-person Houston Bahá'í community. However, they comprise only about 9 percent of Local Spiritual Assembly members. Thus, while young adults are relatively under-represented in positions of "official power" in Bahá'í ecclesiastical governance (members of the LSA or Assistants to Auxiliary Board Members), they occupy positions of status as educators and tutors of youth, which is becoming a more important goal in the last several "Plans" of Bahá'í growth and development. Most children's class teachers and nearly all junior youth tutors are young adults.

Michael McMullen, Ph.D., is associate professor of sociology and cross cultural studies at the University of Houston and a member of the steering committee for the Cooperative Congregational Studies Partnership. He worked for five years at the Martin Luther King Center for Nonviolent Social Change in Atlanta and spent a year as a Fulbright Scholar teaching at the American University in Cairo.

Chapter 6
Kirkwood United Church of Christ
Atlanta, Georgia

By Kristina Lizardy-Hajbi

This case study focuses on Kirkwood United Church of Christ (KUCC), a progressive Protestant Christian community located in the heart of Atlanta's Kirkwood neighborhood. KUCC is a new church, started in 2006 by the Reverend Susannah Davis at a local coffee shop owned by Susannah and her partner Susan.

Considered to be one of the most vibrant new churches in the United Church of Christ (UCC), KUCC has received publicity and financial support from the denomination and was most recently featured in a news story highlighting the congregation's participation in Mission 4/1 Earth, a church-wide effort to bring greater awareness and action on earth care and environmental issues. (United Church News, March 5, 2013) The church also received funding from the UCC's New and Renewing Church Fund, was featured in national promotional materials for this same fund, and has been highlighted in a number of other denominational publications.

The description from the church's website states: "Kirkwood United Church of Christ is a progressive Christian community gathered in the Kirkwood neighborhood of Atlanta and serving our surrounding communities, including East Lake, Oakhurst, Decatur, Edgewood, Candler Park and Grant Park. We are a vibrant congregation that worships together and serves together, that cares about others and seeks to be authentic, and is welcoming of all people. We are actively engaged in our community, living out Jesus' gospel of justice, mercy, love and grace."

The description continues: "God is love, and at Kirkwood UCC we believe God's love belongs to all of us. As a congregation, we strive to open our hearts without fear of seeming different and open our doors to share God's love with the entire community. We not only worship together, but also serve together. We believe in reaching out to those in need, just as we reach out to hold each other up. Above all, we believe in the transformative power of God's love in human hearts. Everyone, Everyone, Everyone is Invited and Welcomed!" (Church Web site)

Data Collection

A three-day site visit to Kirkwood United Church of Christ was conducted in late April 2013. The researcher had the opportunity to participate in a number of activities including a Sunday evening worship service, a community outreach event in conjunction with Mission 4/1 Earth, Soup Saturday community meal, and a young adult gathering. The researcher also engaged in numerous informal conversations with KUCC participants, conducted a focus group with 21 young adults from the congregation, and held in-depth interviews with three key leaders: Davis, KUCC pastor and founder; Mary Kathryn Tippett, coordinator of the young adult group; and Anna Flowers, current seminarian intern and participant in/supporter of the young adult group. In-depth interviews were recorded and transcribed, and extensive notes were taken of the focus group and participant activities.

In addition, thorough reviews of the church's website, promotional/event materials, and other church documents were conducted, as well as a review of denominational and local community materials in which KUCC was featured. All information in this case study originated from data collected during the site visit and from relevant documents.

Description of the Congregation and Key Demographics

The vision and mission of KUCC is as follows: "Worship. Love. Serve." Davis articulated, "If it fits within one of these three areas, that's what we try to be about in an authentic way." The congregation is also committed to radical inclusion in which "everyone, everyone, everyone" is welcome. This includes not only LGBT persons, but persons with whom others may not agree (Davis remarked, "Even people who support Chick-Fil-A because that's the gospel of Jesus").

In total, the number of affiliating individuals at KUCC is around 150; and on average, around 80-90 persons attend the weekly Sunday evening worship service, which occurs at 5:00 p.m. and lasts about an hour. The congregation has grown steadily over the six years of its existence and currently meets in a small, two-story, storefront building in which they are the primary renters.

There are two ways that individuals enter into covenant with the congregation, which is understood and practiced differently than a traditional membership process. As articulated on the KUCC website: "A person in *congregational covenant* is committed to being a full part of the life of the congregation by investing time, talent, service and financial resources, and by being in prayer with and for KUCC. A person in *faith covenant* believes in and chooses to follow Jesus the Christ, will celebrate and participate in the sacraments of baptism and holy communion, promises to grow in the grace and knowledge of God, three in one, and promises to be a witness of God's love in the world in word and deed." About 130 persons have entered into one or both of these covenants (roughly 85 percent of the total church community).

The rectangular shape of the physical space guides the setup, with the center of the rectangle as the focal point for the pulpit, altar table, two small screens, piano, and other musical instruments. Folding chairs turn into the center on either side so that half of the congregation faces the other half. The whole building is divided by a wall, and on the other side of the wall there is a small gathering space for a few tables, a nursery area, kitchen, and bathroom.

Worship is informal, yet follows a traditional Protestant structure. A paper bulletin, as well as a PowerPoint projected on two large monitors, guides the flow of the service. Two acoustic guitars (one played by Davis), a conga, and a string bass lead the music and singing. The opening song for Sunday's worship on the day of the research visit was "Get Together," popularized in the 1960s by The Youngbloods. The Children's Time was a special blessing of the bikes, and anyone (regardless of age) brought their bike helmets forward and sat in the center space. A young adult seminary student led this moment, riding in on a small tricycle. Following this, a simple message was given by Davis, the offering was taken and blessed, prayers and joys were shared (one young adult lesbian couple announced their marriage the previous weekend, with the congregation exploding in cheers and applause), and the closing song was sung ("Hold Us Together" by contemporary Christian artist Matt Maher). Davis describes the worship as "authentic, homegrown, and not slick in any way."

There also are a number of other activities and ministries that occur at KUCC including: A weekly Wednesday morning service of lectionary Bible study, communion, and meditation; small groups such as a liturgical writers' gathering, community garden caretakers, monthly "Wine Down Wednesdays" where people can gather for wine or grape juice and fellowship; and various Bible study series throughout the year. Activities and gatherings are open to all; and there is a great deal of flexibility and fluidity in regard to the type, size, and duration of these activities.

One of the central community outreach ministries of KUCC is Soup Saturday, which has occurred the last two Saturdays of each month for the past three years. Around 11:00 a.m., people in need in the Kirkwood area come to the building to eat a meal. Prior to the start of the meal, Davis drives throughout the neighborhood to areas where transient people are known to gather and announces to folks to "come on over for some food." Davis said, "We usually need to do this in order to remind people that there is food available." Several individuals who benefit from this ministry also routinely help to prepare and serve the food, as well as attend the Sunday evening services and participate in other activities.

In terms of church demographics, roughly 80 percent are white. Other participants identify as non-white with the largest racial demographic being African American, many of whom also participate in Soup Saturday. Davis said this about other demographic indicators: "When we first started [in 2006], we prayed for men. We were mostly female. Now we are 60-40 female to male. We also prayed for more straight people to attend; and now we're 60-40 straight to LGBT folks." The congregation is also economically diverse, with a little less than one-third of people being either very poor or very wealthy. The majority of people, however, are somewhere in the middle-class income range of $30,000-$70,000 per year. Davis remarked, "We are not trying to pretend that we are diverse; but at the outset, we wanted to try to reflect the demographics of our neighborhood. In this way, we are pretty multicultural in the way that Kirkwood is multicultural."

So far as the demographic of age, about 50 percent of the church is in the 30 to 50 age range, which makes them a younger congregation than the average mainline Protestant church. Ten percent is 50 and older, and twenty percent are children and youth 18 and under. This means that roughly 20 percent of the congregation is comprised of young adults (18 to 30), although there is a bit of nuance to this, as many of the young adults are seminarians, as will be shown below.

Community Setting and Congregational History

The neighborhood of Kirkwood and several of the surrounding neighborhoods in that area of Atlanta have experienced a rise in gentrification in recent years. Houses have been purchased and remodeled by middle class and upper middle class families (mostly white); and homes have become unaffordable by lower middle class families and individuals (mostly black) who have historically lived in the area. A stark contrast, however, is still visible in Kirkwood because of the continuing presence of low-income, transient, and homeless African Americans in spite of this gentrification.

It was this setting in which Davis and her partner, Susan, decided to purchase the local coffee shop in the Kirkwood community in 2006. They were both deeply committed to the economic revitalization of the community itself, not only the religious and spiritual nurture of the community. Worship began monthly in the coffee shop, called Gathering Grounds, in 2007; but they quickly outgrew that location and moved to the Kirkwood Community Center in 2008. By the end of 2008, they had also outgrown that space and moved worship to the Old Kirkwood Library, a private residence of one of KUCC's participating families. In late 2009, they moved into their current storefront space; and at the time of this writing they are at a point in which they have outgrown this space and are looking for a building to purchase, with possible financial assistance from the denomination.

Each worship location has intentionally remained in the Kirkwood community to reflect KUCC's ties and commitment to the neighborhood and its people. To this day, many of the special services, such as the Easter Sunrise and Blessing of the Animals, and the planned activities of the church are meant to be community-wide events and occur in a nearby park. Often, KUCC takes out ads in the neighborhood newsletter (Kirkwood Neighbor) and posts fliers around the area.

This particular area of Atlanta is also close to Candler School of Theology, a United Methodist seminary where Davis has taught a contextual education course for the past ten years, and the larger Emory University which has a substantial young adult population. In general, the greater religious context in which KUCC is situated lies within the heart of the "Bible Belt South," where larger, more theologically conservative churches than KUCC draw greater crowds of younger and older adults alike. United Methodist, Baptist, and Presbyterian (PCA) churches reside within the neighborhood; and a couple of new ministries that are particularly targeting young adults have been started in the area, which are also more theologically conservative than KUCC and may/may not be affiliated with a particular denomination.

Young Adults at KUCC

History: Davis described the increase in young adult worshippers at KUCC in this way: "Last year, we had two young adult seminarians who served as interns with us. They invited their friends from seminary to come to church. Then they invited other 20-somethings that lived in Atlanta. One day, I looked up during worship and noticed a bunch of 20-somethings were there! So, I was going out for coffee with all of these young people, inviting them to coffee one by one ... and I wasn't sure what questions to ask. I felt like an old woman, and I'm sure they were thinking that I *was* an old woman!"

In fact, Davis is only 42 at this writing. She started KUCC while still in her 30s, so she is not a great deal older than the young adults in the congregation. This could indeed be a characteristic that is a draw for young adults, although this researcher believes that her charismatic leadership style and her connections with Candler play a larger role in the growth of young adult participants than her own relative youth.

When she realized her young adult cohort was increasing, she met with the two seminarian interns, and together they decided to host a gathering for young adults at Davis and her partner's home, which the congregation refers to as "the parsonage" (though it is their personal home, not owned by the church). The people that were gathered decided to form an informal social group, and the next month they met for a pool party at the interns' apartment complex. In December 2012, the group held a Christmas party where new leadership for the group was chosen since the two seminarians finished their internship earlier that year. These have been the only

117

three "official" events of the young adult group; however, they often walk to Pullman's, a local pub and eatery, following Sunday evening worship. Last year, the group also started a Facebook page; and they maintain contact with one another and announce events through the page.

Understanding the Constituency: It is estimated at this writing that 25-30 young adults (17 to 20 percent of the total congregation) participate in the life of KUCC. However, several individuals in their 30s (up to 35 years old) have also participated in young adult gatherings; so the total number of participants is around 30-35 (20 to 23 percent of the total congregation). The large majority of the group is Euro-American/white. There is a fairly even balance between single individuals and couples, and straight and LGBT young adults. Only a few of the participants have children. Davis stated that families with young children are more common among those in their later 30s and into their 40s.

The most striking characteristic of young adults at KUCC revolves around their education and vocational paths. The group is mostly comprised of graduate students and the spouses of those students (2/3 of the group); but there are a few individuals who are working professionals (1/3 of the group). In particular, KUCC has become a place that attracts young adult seminary students.

The reasons for this vary, but there are a few main factors that contribute to this confluence of young seminarians at KUCC: (1) Davis has served as contextual education faculty at Candler School of Theology for the past decade. She articulated that her presence there as a UCC minister has offered an alternative for seminary students who may be struggling with their sexuality and what it means for their ordination in more theologically conservative denominations. (2) Seminary students who are drawn to the UCC or to Davis and her ministry have invited other seminary students, spouses, and friends in Atlanta to attend KUCC. (3) Seminarians see the ministry of KUCC as a place in which they can participate and develop their skills as future ministers. (4) The congregation, through the guidance of Davis, has embraced its role as a community that trains and sends ministers to serve throughout the denomination.

KUCC currently has nine Members in Discernment (MIDs). (Members in Discernment are individuals who are formally in the process of ordination in the United Church of Christ.) Seven of those nine individuals are young adults in their 20s. In the last couple of years, the church has also trained and ordained two other young adults who are now serving churches in other parts of the country.

It is important to note that not all of the seminary students present at KUCC attend or have attended Candler. Some students have come from Columbia Theological Seminary, a school of the Presbyterian Church (USA) located in nearby Decatur. Of the nine MIDs, only one was raised in the United Church of Christ—the rest were raised in other traditions.

The following activities and processes are in place or have occurred for the MIDs in terms of leadership development: (1) There is a MID Team at the church who meets with all of them and guides them through their process of ordination. Local church teams or committees of this kind are a general requirement for MIDs and are part of the ordination process in the UCC. (2) Once a year, they gather together at "the parsonage" for a cookout. (3) On Shrove Tuesday, Davis gathered with the group to talk about that process of burning ashes; and then they led the Ash Wednesday service as a way to engage in some hands-on, practical training. (4) As previously mentioned, several seminarians have completed their year-long internships with KUCC, which involved leading programs, preaching, and working with Davis on a regular basis. (5) Davis has held many one-on-one conversations with seminarians and offered mentoring, advice, and pastoral presence when needed. (6) All seminarians are encouraged by both Davis and the MID Team to develop their skills and follow their gifts and passions in ways that are most beneficial for them, including participating in leading worship, preaching, and coordinating various initiatives and programs in the church.

At KUCC, the young adult group and the MID group are comprised of many of the same individuals; so there is some degree of overlap. However, the young adults are more inclusive and thus are a larger, more diverse group. Anna Flowers, current KUCC seminarian intern and participant in the young adult group, reflected on this overlap by articulating, "If you have a good group of seminarians at your church, it's a feeder to attract other young adults. What a way to kick-start a young adult ministry by putting 'muscle' behind working with young religious leaders! I think it would be a lot harder to build a young adult group without this."

Since seven individuals are identified as seminarian Members in Discernment, this translates to roughly 20 to 25 percent of the total young adult group. The 75 to 80 percent of the young adults who are not seminarians fall into three other categories: other graduate students, spouses of graduate students/seminarians, and single working professionals. A few individuals are enrolled in masters programs at various schools in the Atlanta area, with individuals working toward degrees in social work, nursing, teaching, or liberal arts. Davis said, "There are no business or engineering students." The spouses of these students (if they have spouses or partners) tend to have entry- or mid-level professional positions in their chosen fields of training such as IT or teaching. The single working professionals hold similar positions.

The church is still growing and the young adult group is not a fully structured program, so it is most common that young adults have participated in the overall life of the church and have served in the places of leadership that the church offers and cultivates. One young individual served as the coordinator for KUCC's Mission 4/1 Earth initiative, many regularly lead various aspects of worship and also preach (usually seminarians), some facilitate or participate in small groups and

Bible studies, and some create their own projects and initiatives within the church and community depending on their passions.

This spirit of leadership and participation is not exclusive to the seminarians in the group, either. Young adults are present throughout all programs and activities of the congregation and are incorporated into the whole life of the church in this way. One male in his early 30s remarked, "I co-lead a weekly Bible study. My graduate degree is in English, but Susannah thought that my attention to literary criticism would be a gift for the group. I have to say that I've really enjoyed helping to lead the study."

Because young adults intentionally occupy many different leadership positions and participate in all activities of the church, they have also developed intergenerational relationships at KUCC. Flowers said this: "When I was at [another church] in Atlanta, they were much more established. But it was also kind of like the young adults were their own group and were not integrated with the whole church. KUCC is the opposite of that church. You want integration. We [young adults] are part of the church—it is a different kind of community here." According to Davis, some of the older adults have also taken some young adults "under their wing" and have invited them out to meals, drinks, or over to their homes.

Budget and Finances

Because KUCC is a new congregation, there is no designated budget for young adult ministries in particular. However, if a need arises and it is reasonable financially, it would be possible for the group to request and receive funding. At this point, all activities have been paid for individually; and they have intentionally held gatherings that are low cost to both the individual and the group. Mary Kathryn Tippet, coordinator of the young adult group and a working professional stated: "For now, we are just looking for fun social activities that don't cost much. We've talked about hiking, going out for beer, etc. I really think you have to start it out as a social group to get people involved, and then you can build from there."

Underlying Philosophy/Theology

While an underlying philosophy/theology for young adult ministry has not been specifically developed, the overall values and principles that support and guide KUCC in general are deeply integral to the structure and approach of the young adult community within the church. This philosophy/theology includes the following themes.

1. *Worship. Love. Serve.* These three words undergird all ministries, activities, and relationships of the church, particularly as they are related to the physical commitment of the congregation to be present and serve the neighborhood of Kirkwood and surrounding areas.

2. *Everyone. Everyone. Everyone!* This highlights the full inclusion of all persons into the life of the church. KUCC has embraced the motto of the denomination that, "No matter who you are or where you are on life's journey, you are welcome here." This has also translated into a *sense of belonging* that young adults expressed as being present in the church community.

3. *Authenticity.* One of the guiding belief statements on KUCC's website is, "We believe that we are called to be real, honest, and authentic." This is the single most important theme that leaders and young adults articulated as a core value of the ministry. Anna offered some poignant thoughts about this value: "I think we are really authentic. We are not doing this in a smarmy way, but we really are because we live it. What you see is what you get. Susannah has been firm with me that we don't want to be a 'slick church,' so we've found a beautiful balance between doing something nice with care and still being authentic. The other new, hip church in our area, Resonate, has a website that looks like a night club. It's so slick—we are trying something different here. My brother-in-

law came to this church when he was living with us—he has lots of drug issues—but he was moved by this child who is blind and disabled but is free to play music with the worship group. He came home with us and said that that is how church is supposed to be."

4. *Faithfulness and flexibility.* The congregation and the leadership are committed to making the church work for the people, not the other way around, according to Susannah. Their philosophy of "church is not a business" opens new possibilities for creativity and meeting the needs of the church and local community in ways that more established churches may not be able to do.

Key Dynamics for Success with Young Adults

Several dynamics were identified in the course of conversations, interviews, and focus groups with young adults and church leaders that were central to the overall success of this ministry within the congregation. Some of these dynamics overlapped with the underlying philosophies of KUCC. Below are brief descriptions of these themes, along with excerpts of conversations with several young adults in the church.

1. *Sense of openness / welcome / inclusion / belonging:* One element that is clear from talking with people at KUCC is that they feel welcomed and comfortable, regardless of their backgrounds and experiences. They appreciate the explicitness of this message and the ways in which inclusion is practiced throughout the life of the congregation. This translates into individuals feeling a sense of belonging (and ownership) within the community. One young adult remarked: "I get a consistent message from the congregation and Susannah. I grew up Methodist and was looking for a church, but the messages at other churches were always mixed—the pastor would be welcoming, but the people non-welcoming…or vice versa. This is especially true as a gay person. One pastor just assumed my partner and I were sisters, and they wouldn't believe otherwise." A newcomer to

KUCC and the young adult group emphasized this dynamic: "I've been looking for a church for three years, and this is only my fourth time at KUCC. Each time, someone has spoken to me. That's huge!"

This sense of welcome and openness not only extends to sexuality, but also to openness regarding theological commitments: "I've been trying to figure out who I am as an adult and hadn't been in a church in three years. But my first week at Kirkwood, I felt it was a place where everyone is welcome and I can be questioning. And if I wanted guidance—which I don't right now—it would be there." Another young adult mentioned, "Having the kind of openness to people along the faith spectrum—for example, the different covenants and faith memberships—is a huge draw. It also allows a lot of couples who are in different places in their faith journeys to be here."

This does not mean, however, that openness to individuals of different sexual orientations and identities isn't important for young adults. One seminarian said, "For me a church has to be Open and Affirming. It matters to my husband too. KUCC is a place where I can bring my sister and her girlfriend. And it matters in the city of Atlanta." ("Open and Affirming" is the designation for churches in the United Church of Christ that choose to be welcoming of all persons, particularly LGBT persons.) One young woman also shared that "as a Republican, I'm not defined by this at KUCC. I don't feel shunned because of it. You are part of the group here."

2. Commitment to authenticity / honesty / realness: As one of the other main dynamics that has contributed to the overall success of KUCC and the young adult growth within the congregation, the commitment to authenticity is reflected throughout all practices and interactions. As plainly articulated by one young seminarian, "I like that we drink at Easter brunch—it's honest, and we're not pretending. It's not dress-up."

Anna Flowers, the current intern at KUCC, talked about the ways in which other communities in the area are not as authentic and honest in their messaging and approach as KUCC: "I have many anecdotes of other young progressive Christians who find themselves at very conservative churches unbeknownst to them. There is a failure of communication and lack of transparency there. The atmosphere could be progressive culturally, but it is very conservative theologically and socially. They should be coming here." This authenticity plays into KUCC's commitment to inclusion and welcome as well, in order to meet people where they are in their own theological and life journeys. "I don't have it all figured out, and it's a process," said one young adult male. "I don't know about this Jesus, but I know this community. The door is open to just come in, whoever you are. That's real and reflects where a lot of young adults are at." Another individual said, "A lot of churches have the 'gay' thing, and that's the one thing they're about. There's more to KUCC than that. It didn't need to be proclaimed because it is understood. I appreciated the authenticity in that." In terms of practice and messaging, it is evident that this theme is present throughout both elements.

3. Shared participation and ownership as intentional leadership development: Participants in the life of KUCC not only feel that they are welcomed and included in the community; they also feel a sense of ownership in the ministry and the outcomes of the congregation. There is a spirit of openness to co-creating the present and future mission and vision; and young adults in particular expressed that they feel their gifts are celebrated, nurtured, and utilized. One young woman remarked, "I love KUCC because the leadership and Susannah have always said, 'Come and create with me.' Everyone has a hand in what's going on. If you are into bikes or if you're good with kids, your skill set can be a part of the whole and you can contribute."

Another person reflected, "Over the years, I've watched ideas grow and develop into things people have ownership of. That's a huge gift. Instead of being told what to do and how to live, you can actually see your own gifts and philosophies about life develop."

This dynamic has been intentionally created by the leadership of the community. "When I first met with Susannah for coffee, she talked with me about how KUCC was a place where there was room for me to be who I am and to share my gifts with others while growing and serving at the same time," said one young adult.

Another young adult summarized this dynamic best by articulating, "With more traditional churches, you get swept into the work of doing church. Compared to how much effort other churches ask of you, it's nothing here. It's lean and mean. I throw my weight into something. It's not the maintenance of structures—it's co-creating and co-participating."

4. Charismatic leadership paired with purposeful relationship building: It is apparent that the leadership of Davis has been, and continues to be, a key dynamic in the growth and vitality of the congregation. In addition, Susannah's role in shaping and modeling the central philosophies of KUCC through the building of intentional relationships has greatly influenced young adults in the community and seminarian young adults in particular. One young woman said, "Susannah is a big reason I came at the beginning. The first time I came, she ran down the street to meet me after the service."

A young seminary student quipped, "The pastor matters a lot. We love Susannah, and we believe in the mission." May Kathryn, coordinator of the young adult group, said the following in regard to talking about the growth and vitality of the congregation: "Some of it has to do with Susannah, and she is a good role model for people. It takes a special person to start a new church."

One particular young female also talked about the long-standing relationship she has had with Davis. "When I was

12," she said, "I was baptized by Susannah at a very conservative church where she was a pastor at the time. As a teen, I was always asking where Susannah was after she left that church. She did a funeral for a friend of my mom's a couple of years ago; and I was so excited I had found her that I cried!"

A significant part of the charismatic leadership and purposeful relationship building has occurred through Davis and her partner's use of their personal home, "the parsonage." One young adult said, "Susan and Susannah host a lot at the parsonage. After Easter we had a brunch thing. Their dinner parties help us to intentionally meet other people. Susannah is very intentional about us meeting one another. Not a lot of other churches do this. Susannah plays 'matchmaker' for the people in the church to build relationships."

5. *Integration of young adults with the whole congregation / intergenerational interaction:* While there is a group of young adults who have been gathering on and off for the past year, young adults ultimately see this group of peers as secondary to their presence and participation in the larger congregation. They value relationships with others in the church as much as relationships with their generational peers. A young adult male said, "We don't want to be set up solely by our affinity group. It is intentional that KUCC is set up by what ministries people want to be a part of." Another young person commented, "There are a lot of older couples that I look up to at KUCC— they give me positive examples of what it's like to be in partnership with someone else."

This type of intergenerational relating and fellowship is important for many young adults in the community, particularly because of the transient nature of this age group. "Not everyone will stay in Atlanta for a long time, which is common," said one individual. "But I feel like it is a little bit of a family away from home. Older folks always pay for a drink or a meal when we go out, which is nice." One young adult even suggested, "The 60-somethings should merge with us [the young adult group]!" (Bear in mind that, as noted above, only ten percent of this congregation is over 50.)

6. Focus on community-based ministry: Through Davis's leadership, this dynamic has become an important factor for several of the young adults and their participation in the activities of KUCC. "The grounding of the church within the community is important," responded one young woman. "It's not separate from the space in which it exists. Part of that is Susannah who knows and lives in the community; part of that is the congregation that cares for the community and people moving there to be a part of the place. Community is important to me. Lots of churches donate but don't really know the community." One couple even said, "We are moving to Kirkwood because of Susannah and the community."

For these young adults, being a part of a ministry that is contextual possesses an element of authenticity and meaning for them. One individual stated, "We don't even live in Kirkwood, but we stand behind the fact that this is a community ministry. It exists for its locality. Localized ministry is what people my generation are looking for. If you are at all religious, the movement now is to make it local. We've looked to moving here, but it's not feasible for us."

7. Attractive online presence: While this particular factor may not be a central reason that young adults have remained at KUCC, it seems to be a dynamic that has drawn several young adults to the church in the first place. A young woman said, "The website attracted me the first time. It's a very good website. All of the events KUCC was involved in were there, and it was put together well and was informative." Another individual talked about how she came to learn about the church. "I had always been online looking at different churches; then Kirkwood UCC popped up on the web. There were no good places that were UCC in Atlanta, but this was different. I was kind of stalking KUCC online for a couple of months, then I came with my sister."

Because of the increased young adult presence and participation within the church, this population is also taking ownership of ways that KUCC can have a more engaging, technologically savvy presence online. For example, Anna has just launched a new online platform for the church called "The City." The goal of the platform is to share about church and community events and better connect people to one another. Flowers said, "Hopefully, it will also be a way that we attract more young adults to our community, as well as better connect the group that we have. I'm excited about trying this new way of interacting."

Broader Meaning and Generalizability of the KUCC Case

Kirkwood United Church of Christ possesses several characteristics that the overall Faith Communities Today (FACT) research identified as typical for churches with larger numbers of young adults. First, new congregations like KUCC that were formed recently are more likely to attract younger adults. As articulated in a recent FACT publication, "Those groups organized in 2000 or later are more than three times as likely to have an above-average number of young adults as those organized before 1976." (*Faith Communities Today Newsletter*, Issue 19, January 2013)

Second, KUCC is located in an urban neighborhood of Atlanta; and congregations with significant young adult populations are more than twice as likely located in urban or suburban areas as in small towns or rural areas.

Third, KUCC uses technology in fairly significant ways. As articulated by recent FACT research, "There is a clear correlation between use of technology by congregations and engaging with young adults. Nearly one in four of the congregations that make major use of new technology have exceptional numbers of young adults." (*Ibid.*) While KUCC may not always make major use of online technology in the ways that larger congregations have the resources to do, they are moving toward incorporating technology into the church's overall activities and relationships through implementation of "The City."

Fourth, KUCC has a number of programs and activities to engage young adults in their ministry, which is another similar characteristic of congregations identified in the FACT study.

And fifth, worship at KUCC, while possessing elements common to a traditional mainline Protestant order of worship, was executed in a contemporary style. The use of guitars and a drum, as well as projection equipment, were elements lifted up by FACT researchers as correlating more strongly with congregations with young adults.

There are also a few characteristics that make KUCC somewhat of a unique case when compared with congregations highlighted in the FACT research. The congregation is somewhat small with only 150 participants in total. According to FACT data, while there is not a strong relationship between the presence of young adults and larger congregations, there is a slight relationship between these two factors. It is important to note, however, that KUCC continues to grow in number; so this characteristic may change over time.

In addition, the presence of a solo full-time pastor at KUCC is unique for a growing presence of young adults, as "a solo full-time clergy leader is significantly less likely than two or more full-time clergy or no full-time clergy" to lead this type of congregation. (*Ibid.*) However, Davis's direct connection with Candler School of Theology, as well as the close proximity of at least two seminaries to the church itself, counters this characteristic. In essence, KUCC might also be considered a multiple-staff church with the presence of interns, which most likely contributes to the significant growth in the young adult population as well.

Over and above these fairly quantifiable similarities and differences to FACT-identified churches, it is critical to stress the overall thematic dynamics that have contributed to KUCC's success in attracting and retaining its young adult population. Several key dynamics are comparable to those highlighted in preliminary case study research conducted by FACT, some of which are as follows: (1) Experienced or charismatic leadership. (2) Casual informality; experimental and experiential quality. (3) Quality experiences, but not wanting an emphasis on quality to lead to inauthentic worship or prevent experimentation. (4) Participatory activity. (Chang)

These four dynamics found in other case studies to date are reflected in KUCC's themes of a commitment to authenticity/honesty/realness, shared participation and ownership as intentional leadership development, and charismatic leadership paired with purposeful relationship building. Davis is both an experienced and charismatic leader of KUCC, and her commitment to creating an authentic community is soundly evidenced. In many ways, the casual informality experienced in other settings correlates to that sense of authenticity which KUCC emphasizes. The presence of experimentation and participatory activity correlates with the shared participation and ownership that Davis and others in the congregation invite people to explore in order to cultivate and utilize gifts for leadership development.

There are, however, a few key dynamics that this case study highlights which were not previously identified, but may be important elements in deepening an understanding of young adult ministry. First, cultivating openness, welcome, inclusion, and belonging in ministry for young adults is a critical factor in KUCC's success. This is translatable to other congregations, as increasing numbers of young people view religion in general, and church specifically, as simplistic and judgmental on issues of sexuality, exclusive, and unfriendly to doubters. (Barna) KUCC's consistency between its beliefs and practices of including "everyone, everyone, everyone" seems to be a defining dynamic for the retention and growth of the young adult population and the congregation as a whole.

Second, while there are some specific young adult activities in the church, integration of young adults with the whole congregation in intergenerational interaction seems to be an important dynamic that is contributing to KUCC's success. Rather than being seen as a demographic to be targeted, other congregations might focus energies articulating and carrying out the core philosophies of the church for the benefit of all members, but in ways that could also appeal to young adults' desires for authenticity/ informality and participatory activity. Because KUCC is a small but growing congregation, it does not possess the finances or the staff to underwrite and support ministries based on particular demographics. If the congregation were to gain those resources, however, it would alter that nature of the overall ministry. This dearth of resources could be good news for smaller congregations that want to attract young adults to their churches.

Third, KUCC's focus on community-based ministry reflects a desire for authenticity and connection in a different, but important way than other congregations might currently envision in their ministries. It also reflects the desire for participatory, experiential activity among young adults rather than a more traditional model of charity and programming that may be present in other churches and that may have been the practice among older generations within the church.

While no singular set of characteristics can determine increases in the presence of young adults in any congregation, Kirkwood United Church of Christ offers a model of ministry and engagement with younger adults that contributes to the scholarship and collection of best practices on the subject. It is the hope that some of the findings provided in this case study will be beneficial for those who are looking to include and invite this particular generation into their places of worship.

Rev. Kristina Lizardy-Hajbi, Ph.D., serves as director of the Research Center in the United Church of Christ. She is also an adjunct faculty member at Iliff School of Theology in Denver, Colorado.

References

Barna Research Group. "Six Reasons Young Christians Leave Church." September 28, 2011, www.barna.org/teens-next-gen-articles/528-six-reasons-young-christians-leave-church.

Chang, Perry, "Wider Support, Location Key for Success: Case Studies Identify Critical Factors for Young Adult Ministries," Faith Communities Today, August 2012.

Church Web site, www.kirkwooducc.com

Faith Communities Today Newsletter, Issue 19, January 2013.

United Church News, "Atlanta Church Pairs Partnerships and Projects for Mission 4/1 Earth," *United Church News*, March 5, 2013; http://www.ucc.org/news/atlanta-church-pairs.html.

Documentation related to Kirkwood UCC

"Atlanta Church Pairs Partnerships and Projects for Mission 4/1 Earth," *United Church News*, March 5, 2013,
http://www.ucc.org/news/atlanta-church-pairs.html

"New Atlanta Church Dares to Embrace Big Mission:1 Goals," *United Church News*, November 3, 2011,
http://www.ucc.org/news/new-atlanta-church-dares-to.html

"'Suncoast Saturday' Ends with Celebration of Possibilities," *United Church News*, July 2, 2011,
http://www.ucc.org/news/suncoast-saturday-ends-with.html

2010 Strengthen the Church Offering Bulletin Inserts:
http://www.ucc.org/stc/pdf/stc-2010/STC-2010-Printable-Insert-B-Kirkwood.pdf

"Discernment and Training for Church Planting and Redevelopment," *United Church News*, June/July 2009, http://www.ucc.org/ucnews/june-july-2009/discernment-and-training-for.html

"Gathering Grounds for Kirkwood United Church of Christ," *UCC New Times*, Summer 2007, p. 5, http://www.ucc.org/newchurch/pdfs/ucc-nt-summer-2007.pdf

Chapter 7
Life Center Foursquare Church
Spokane, Washington

By Tamara Michalenko Terry

The 80,000 square foot Life Center Foursquare Church at 1202 N Government Way, Spokane, Washington, may seem more like a hotel on first entering. Its lobby includes a wall of windows, a coffee bar, and an area with enough space for kids to play games that are a part of their programs. It is affiliated with the International Church of the Foursquare Gospel.

The church's information brochure describes the goal as creating a living room setting. "We want you to feel at home and linger." The coffee bar provides complimentary coffee and tea with espresso drinks available for a donation for "mission activities at home and around the world." Unlike most churches, attendees are encouraged to take the drinks into the sanctuary to enjoy during the service. *The Spokesman-Review* reporter Kelly McBride wrote in a November 12, 1995, article that Life Center "goes through more Starbucks than a small diner." She also noted that "the congregation downs at least 600 cups during the traditional fellowship hour on Sunday mornings." Currently, the church budgets about $800 a month for the warm beverage, but feels it is important to the relaxed atmosphere and fellowship.

In its 1800-seat sanctuary, Life Center has three Sunday services at 9 a.m., 11:15 a.m., and 5 p.m. The services are scheduled for one hour and 15 minutes. Children's programming for birth through 5th grade is offered during most service times with youth and young adult programs available on different days of the week. Life Center provides several levels of children's ministries: AdventureLand Kids, birth to age 5, Roots, age 6-8, and Mosaic, age 9-12.

The first service demographics are usually older. The second service is rather mixed age-wise while the evening service is much younger. Some would consider the praise portion of the service to be similar to a rock concert as a full band leads attendees through a variety of contemporary songs while baptisms, offerings, and prayer time takes place. Three screens enable everyone to see what is happening on the stage. Within minutes of the beginning of the service, a question is suggested for attendees to ask those around them, giving them the ice breaker needed to talk to someone new.

When prayer time comes, instead of someone leading prayer from the pulpit, attendees are given several minutes to reflect on a question from the worship coordinator that goes along with the service theme.

Rather than scheduling a service specifically for youth and young adults, this sort of service is intended to include any age. In addition, many in that age group assist with the service in areas of music, video, sound, or helping in the children's divisions.

Joe Wittwer is the lead pastor and preaches 90 to 95 percent of the time. David Lewellyn, Matt Clark, and Michael Hockett are also speaking pastors and team leaders, coordinating different aspects of the church. Life Center has a staff of more than 40 with countless volunteers assisting in a variety of ministries. Their church theme is "Loving God, Loving People." The service is offered in English and American Sign Language.

"Life Center is dedicated to helping people become whole-hearted followers of Christ," their website states. "By following Christ's example, we can make a difference in the lives of others and in our community."

Their goal is to reach 10 percent of Spokane County by 2020. Spokane's population in 2010 was 208,916. The average median age is 35. The estimated median household income in 2009 was $38,939. Whites make up 84 percent of the population with Hispanics at 5 percent. Statistics show men and women in Spokane pretty equal with males at 48.8 percent and women at 51.2 percent. A March 2012 statistic put the cost of living index for Spokane at 92.9, less than the national average at 100. A look at ancestries found German to be the highest at 22.9 percent. Irish was next at 13.8 percent followed by English at 12.1 percent. For the population of 25 or older, 88.1 percent had a high school or higher degree. In Spokane 36.1 percent are affiliated with a religious congregation. The breakdown shows attendees for the Catholic Church at 39 percent, Presbyterian Church at 5 percent and other at 35 percent. (City-data.com)

History/Vision/Mission

According to official Web site of the International Church of the Foursquare Gospel, "The term 'Foursquare Gospel' came about during an intense revival in the city of Oakland, Calif., in July 1922. To a crowd of thousands, Aimee Semple McPherson explained Ezekiel's vision in the book of Ezekiel, chapter one. Ezekiel saw God revealed as a being with four different faces: a man, a lion, an ox and an eagle. To Sister McPherson, those four faces were like the four phases of the gospel of Jesus Christ. In the face of the man, she saw Jesus our Savior. In the face of the lion, she saw Jesus the mighty Baptizer with the Holy Spirit and fire. In the face of the ox, she saw Jesus the Great Burden-Bearer, who took our infirmities and carried our sicknesses. In the face of the eagle, she saw Jesus the Coming King, who will return in power and victory for the church. It was a perfect, complete Gospel. It was a Gospel that faces squarely in every direction; it was the 'Foursquare Gospel.'"

As a Foursquare Church, the Life Center website states, "we believe Jesus Christ is God's Son, the Savior, Baptizer with the Holy Spirit, the Healer, and the coming King." Their mission is simply, "We think introducing our friends, family, neighbors, and coworkers to Jesus is really important, so we've set some guiding objectives and values to help us stay focused on what matters."

The objectives of Life Center include; (1) Love God with all we've got. (2) Win our neighbors to Jesus. (3) Grow to be all God wants us to be. (4) Send out agents of change into a broken world.

The web site also lists the following values of the congregation. *Prayer:* We pray first! *Relationships:* We believe that loving God and loving people sums up the Christian life. *Authenticity:* We are open, honest, and real. *Simplicity:* We stay centered on Jesus Christ and what He has called us to do. *Excellence:* We do our best for God. *Devotion:* We are wholehearted Christians. *Teamwork:* We value each person's gifts and participation. *Fun:* We enjoy following Jesus!

Life Center Foursquare Church began in Spokane in 1931 as a typical small, Pentecostal church. It remained that way for more than 40 years. Direct from Bible College, Joe Wittwer became lead pastor in May of 1978. "At that time, they gathered at a tiny building near the Spokane County Courthouse, in a church so small that it owned only six off-street parking spots," *The Spokesman-Review* reported on December 12, 2005.

Over the next couple of years attendance increased from roughly 10 or 12 people to more than 300. It was around this time, in 1983-84, that an official youth department began. The congregation had reached about 200 to 225.

"Enough youth attended that Don Crawford was hired to organize a youth group including junior high and high school students," Kafflen said. "College ministry was added a few years later on a volunteer basis and didn't become a paid staff position until moving to the Nora property in the 1990s."

When the Life Center purchased the new facility at 708 W. Nora, they "grew rapidly in numbers and in depth of ministry as staff expanded and teaching matured," stated Bill Kafflen, current assistant executive pastor.

"It's been a wild ride," said Wittwer, referring to the growth of his 1990-1995 weekend attendance from 300 people to 1,800. He was quoted in *The Spokesman-Review* article on Mega-Churches. Staff Writer Kelly McBride stated "What newcomers notice most about these churches is the lack of formality and ritual. Jeans are fine. So are shorts in the summer." And that is just how Life Center wants it, so people are comfortable to come in whatever they are wearing.

"As a generation, we have abandoned the spiritual moorings of our parents," Wittwer continued in *The Spokesman-Review* article. "Then we began having children and marrying and divorcing and facing life as it really is, and there has been an awakening. But that awakening is among a generation that is still fairly anti-institutional. They do not adapt well to traditional churches." A new Gallup survey confirms that statement with only 44 percent expressing confidence in organized religion, down from 68 percent in 1975.

In 2005 Life Center moved to its current location. That move ignited yet another growth spurt and created a "deeper spirituality," Kafflen stated. The church has no formal membership but estimates that 7,000 to 8,000 people in the Spokane area would consider Life Center their church. Sunday service attendance has grown from 3,372 in May 2008 to 4,128 in May 2010, and in May 2012 is at 4,076.

Easter Service

With such a large attendance, church administration had to figure out a way to accommodate the large group that would want to attend an Easter Service and saw renting the Spokane Arena as a way to create a community outreach as well. "Easter is one of those times when people who aren't necessarily members of our congregation will say 'yes' to an invitation, and that's why we do this," Wittner is quoted in an April 17, 2006, article in *The Spokesman-Review*. (Morlin)

In 1996 "5,200 people celebrated Easter in the Spokane Arena," wrote Jamie Tobias Neely in *The Spokesman-Review* article. "It's an opportunity to reach out to the unchurched who aren't in another church," Kafflen stated in the article. "Hopefully, some folks will leave and have a relationship with the Lord." Costs, he estimated, were between $10,000 and $15,000. Neely stated that "the stage was filled with people under 40." During the service she stated that Wittwer "urged the congregation to seek an extraordinary life through Jesus Christ ... 'Life is not about money or power or possessions or self,' he said. 'Your relationships with God and with people are the real riches of life.'"

When *The Spokesman-Review* featured Life Center's 2006 Easter service they estimated that the 7,000-person congregation was "probably the biggest audience in the 10 years Life Center Foursquare Church has been renting the city-owned facility for Easter services," as staff writer Bill Morlin stated in the article. "I've had a lot of people tell me our Easter service was their first church service," Wittwer shared with Morlin for the article. Morlin also mentioned Wittwer led the service "in a Hawaiian print shirt and Dockers slacks."

"Easter is an annual reminder to us that God always has the last word," Wittwer shared in his Easter message. "It's so good to know we're in the Master's hands." Twenty-five Life Center volunteers started at 2 a.m. Sunday to create a "closed-circuit television system with cameras and a high-tech sound system," Morlin reported.

In 2008 organizers moved the services back to their church location and offered five services for Easter and Christmas. "With expenses increasing to almost $30,000, it made more fiscal sense to move back," Kafflen stated. The church had all the technology in place so now they budget about $11,000 and many times don't even spend that much. The 2012 Easter service had 8,454 adults and 1,440 children participate in the services.

Life Groups

Getting connected is an important part of their success. "We really have to work hard at maintaining that sense of community," Wittwer said in *The Spokesman-Review*. (McBride) "You find people shopping for churches based on a personal checklist," Wittwer stated in an article printed the same year by *The Spokesman-Review* on Mega-Churches. "When in fact there's a reciprocity in a biblical community. It's not enough to be a taker. You have to be a giver, too. And not just money."

That philosophy is what started the Life Center Life Groups. "A Life Group," their information brochure explains, "is comprised of three or more people who meet together regularly for friendship and spiritual growth in Christ. They provide an excellent way to live out our mission and the commands Christ gives us in Matthew 27:37-39—love God and love people."

"Life Groups are designed for connection through shared interest, similar life stages, and the opportunity to build friendships," the brochure stated. "Volunteering in a ministry will also help you connect, and is a great way to meet people, and discover more of how God has gifted you."

The church offers a daily reading guide each quarter enabling everyone, including the Life Groups, to have a scripture to focus on. The church staff encourages the SOAP approach. **Scripture:** Read the Bible. **Observation:** What does it mean? **Application:** What does it mean to me? **Prayer:** Pray it back to God.

With more than 200 Life Groups to choose from, meeting in various area locations, attendees are bound to find something that fits their circumstances. The goal is to keep groups small and relaxed, so once a group has a good number of people coming regularly it will "close" so as to not to get too big. For college-age attendees there were at the time of this writing three Life Groups listed that were currently open for new members: a Women's Bible Study, a Girlfriends in God Luncheon/Bible Study, and a Topical Bible Study.

"Moving to emphasize small group settings for the sake of relationship and discipleship has been the most significant change in recent history," Kafflen stated. "Change was made to invigorate personal growth for the participants and young adult ministry as a whole. It has been very successful and therefore we maintain it. The Life Groups have grown from 15 percent to 80 percent in the past five years." All church staff and Life Group leaders are trained and vetted with background checks both locally and nationally.

Pam Craig coordinates one of the college Life Groups. She will readily admit this was not her choice. She felt the Lord calling her to help. When she told Bobby Moore, Life Center college pastor, that she was willing to help where needed, he encouraged her to be a mentor for a Life Group. So she gave up one of the three Life Groups she was attending and started a college-age women's Bible study.

"We started meeting at the church, then at one of the girls' house," Craig shared. "Now we meet in my home. I prepare and serve a meal for the girls, sometimes just salad and healthy snacks. Until I started meeting in my home the group was never larger than three." Now the group averages six or seven, but has been up to 12.

"There have been times when only one showed in these past seven years," Craig admits. "At first I can't pretend that it didn't bother me, but then I learned that the Lord has a plan for me to have exclusive time with the one. Those have been some of the most fruitful meetings for me and them!"

She has learned that a formal approach of study has not worked. "These young women need the support of each other, prayer and encouragement in their daily walks and the structure just becomes a burden," She has found keeping it casual, supportive, and open to sharing what we are going through in life while focusing on growing closer to the Lord, following the leading of the Holy Spirit, and praying for each other is the best formula for the group. "I still take lessons from discipleship classes, but it is in sound bites sandwiched between a fresh garden salad, (most are starved for fresh home cooked food), and prayers for jobs, schools, family, and relationships."

Texting is the number one way of communication with the group, including prayer requests during the week. Facebook is number two. The students average about 1.5 years in her Life Group as they move, get married, graduate, start careers, or go back home. Many have stayed in contact though. Since then, she has helped coordinate a Life Group for college-aged women struggling with sexual pasts. She encourages others to start college-age Life Groups "as long as it is HIS idea and you love the age group."

Mike Beacham coordinates a college-age topical Bible study Life Group that started almost two years before this writing. Enjoying the different Bible stories from the Life Group he was attending, he didn't want the study to end just because leadership changed or life happened. He went through the Life Center training classes and started his own Life Group. Since then, they have studied different books of the Bible, different topical studies such as love, faith, and trust, and world religion units.

"When the group was struggling the most is when we were trying to push certain ideas the hardest, or get the group to go in a direction that people weren't ready to go," Beacham shared. "Especially with younger people, everyone is at a different level of understanding, and you can't work on too high of a level or too low of a level, but really shift between the two. If people aren't able to relate to what you're saying to them, they don't follow along and that removes their level of interest in the group."

Beacham prefers to engage the individuals and challenge them to think about their answers. "Currently, our group's method of engaging people is each week someone different is presenting on a religion. Our hope is to help everyone get a little more comfortable talking about faith in an open setting where they are doing the leading of the conversation, and also to make everyone feel a little more aware of the differences between ourselves and those of other 'faiths.'"

"The thing I've noticed while having a small group is that almost anyone will come to a Bible study, and they'll probably listen. The hard thing is to get them to ask the questions they're afraid to ask, and even harder still is to answer them without driving them away. With new people, it's hard to gauge where they are in their faith, and without a decent amount of chatting outside of a once-a-week, hour(ish)-long meeting, you'll be hard pressed to figure out where they really are, and what the hiccups they are experiencing really are. Those hiccups are what keep people from coming back, because they don't understand one thing, so they feel like they can't get any of it, and therefore none of it must be valid." Beacham's group averages seven to eight people each week.

LouAnn Hommel felt "a strong urging from God" to start a group on the Eastern Washington University campus where she works. She found several Christian staff members and started the group to pray for those who had lost their job due to university "cut-backs." They started meeting twice a month, every first and third Wednesday at noon for an hour.

 "We started as a prayer group, but very soon changed to a study group," she shared. "In the beginning, we decided on a topic and everyone studied the topic on their own and brought it back to the group." They did that for about six months then someone recommended they study a book together. They have studied books ever since. "I didn't start the group with any pre-conceived ideas. I was just trying to obey God's prompting. So I've been completely open to letting the group morph."

146

They do not have the same people show up every time. "Just when I think hardly anyone will be there I am surprised to find a nice-size group of attendees that haven't come in awhile. I am very transparent and have no problem sharing my own personal struggles. As a result, everyone feels free to share. The discussions are lively and engaging. Everyone talks and shares which I love."

She used to accommodate people's schedules, but found that did not work as it always left some people out. She has stuck with the same day and time and enjoys whoever comes. Her highest number of people has been 15, but they average six to eight at a time. For those thinking of starting a small group, she shared, "Don't wait until you think you know enough. If you believe God is prompting you to do it ... do it. He'll work it out."

Young Adult Ministries

ALIVE is a ministry specifically for those 18-25 years of age. They meet every Thursday at 7 p.m. in the church multi-purpose room for a night of worship and teaching in a large group setting. Food is served every time. In the summer, organizers like to barbecue to give the backyard feel for this group. Other times it might be pizza or hot dogs. The college-age students gather and mingle until the band begins. This signals the beginning of the 30-40 minute program filled with contemporary music performed by a full band followed by a speaker. The program always ends with some type of interaction or commitment, a way to respond to what has been said. Occasionally it will be a traditional "alter call," but it could be simply a song of encouragement. The energy in the group is very positive and most leave energized and encouraged for the upcoming week. No offering is taken, as expenses are covered by the church budget.

ALIVE has been meeting since 2007. It started out with about 60 people and has seen steady growth, mostly through word of mouth. They don't advertise but encourage promotion as exemplified by the story of Jesus' disciple, Andrew, calling his brother, Simon: **Find** someone, **Tell** them about the program, and **Bring** them. The current attendance ranges from 120-180, stated Josh Schiel, student ministries Life Groups pastor.

Schiel is also involved in Soul Punch videos created for the specific purpose of making people laugh. "As Christians, we take our faith seriously; in fact we cannot take it too seriously," the website states. "It's when we start taking ourselves too seriously that we get into trouble. And sometimes you just gotta laugh. And sometimes it's at yourself." Schiel explained that the videos are not meant to be disrespectful. "Jesus is fun and we need to celebrate that." Soul Punch videos can be found on the church website or on their You Tube Channel,. "Soul Punch Productions." The videos are produced at random times, with whatever they feel like presenting.

David Lewellyn, Life Center student ministries team leader, stated their practical philosophy is "to help every college-age person in the Spokane area become a whole-hearted, passionate follower of Jesus who will positively impact his/her family, school, church, community, and world now and in the future."

"As young people mature and decisions are made we raise the bar and show them how they can change the world and be empowered by the word of God," Schiel said. Peer leadership is a strong component of the program, as a peer can influence someone more positively than an older person might.

Even though the ALIVE program had not yet officially begun, a June 29, 1995, post by *The Spokesman-Review* announced a picnic sponsored by Life Center for single college students and Twentysomethings after its 9:00 a.m. and 11:00 a.m. Sunday services. That showed interest in that age group long before the programs were formalized.

On February 1, 2010, Life Center ALIVE joined the Facebook craze to promote their events and post photos and videos. The page is geared for the targeted age group and speaks in a language that age group would find entertaining. The diversity of its "Friends" shows that the program appeals to all types of people. At the time of this writing, the page had 532 "Friends. It can be found at "LifeCenter Alive." They also use twitter to promote events and updates.

The young adult ministry staff consists of David Lewellyn, Life Center student ministries team leader, Bobby Moore, Life Center college pastor (Moore is the only full-time person; the rest of the staff divide their time between other age groups), Josh Schiel, Life Center student ministries Life Groups pastor, and Emily Lewellyn, Life Center student ministries support.

When asked if there are any challenges, Lewellyn mentions the difficulty in retaining new believers. "We may not always know why they leave and wish there was something we could do to help but they don't always feel comfortable letting us know they are struggling with something."

College Housing

"College house is an awesome opportunity to grow with God and others in fellowship and community," the College Housing website states. "These homes have anywhere from four to eight roommates and are hubs for ALIVE events, Bible studies, and more. ... The college houses provide an organic culture of meeting people and growing together in faith through reading the Bible, praying, serving, and giving, and then sharing with others," said Lewellyn. Emphasis is placed on excellence in our services (good worship and teaching). Life Center has "six college houses, with one more coming soon, of students who serve, lead, and live in the community with accountability to Godly lives," stated Kafflen.

The houses are owned by individuals and rented to the students. "The church does not deal with any of the financial matters. The lease is between the owner and the student," Lewellyn stated. The church simply helps fill the houses with college-age students looking for a positive environment. There is no alcohol allowed on the premises and the houses are used for many Life Groups, parties, and other young adult events. Even though there is an application available on the church website, Lewellyn said that they are mainly filled by word of mouth. The current houses are called The PAD, The Walton House, Woodside, The Shack, The Ardmore House and The Nook.

Leaders say that college housing has been a huge tool in the discipleship of many. While it is not as formal as a ministry institute or discipleship program, simply living in community together and having weekly house meetings has been very beneficial for many individuals, and therefore, the ministry. The lives of some troubled young people have been transformed by living in a Life Center college house. Lewellyn said they have had to evict people, but only after many, many opportunities have been given to improve.

The houses also host Bible studies, worship nights, barbecues, and parties. Many have had their first encounter with the college ministry at an event such as these. "The discipleship and evangelism aspects of the houses are invaluable to our ministry," said Llewellyn. "Also, the involvement of many college-aged individuals leading in the junior high and senior high programs bolsters the overall involvement in the college community."

Church Plants

Life Center thrives on starting church plants. They feel it is one of the most effective ways to introduce people to a relationship with Christ. They've encouraged 200-600 people from Life Center to become members of church plants in different areas of Spokane. Experienced Life Center staff goes with the members to support the plant. "They know our DNA," Kafflen stated, "so it makes it easier to reproduce what we know works."

Several of the churches started by Life Center include Eastpoint, Garland, Life Center North, Liferoads, Summit Ridge, and West Central. Eastpoint and Garland are not part of the foursquare church but have chosen to be independent organizations. West Central is not technically a church yet as they need 35 people to sign a charter to become a church. Mosaic is a church Life Center helped start. Wittwer meets with all pastors quarterly to discuss common goals and challenges. It is interesting to note that they don't meet in a typical church setting and several focus specifically on college-age and young adults. Below are brief histories of several of these churches.

Eastpoint: "Eastpoint Church is a non-denominational daughter church of Life Center in Spokane, WA. We held our first services in January of 2003. The actual beginning was with a core group of about 90 people who started to meet in October of 2002. Eastpoint experienced explosive growth in our first year and quickly outgrew our initial facility on Argonne. After searching and looking at many different options in the valley, we finally leased 35,000 square feet of the old K-Mart building at the corner of Sullivan and Sprague, which is where we are today. The facility has been ideal for the growth that God has given us and now accommodates nearly 1200 people on the weekends."

Life Center North: "Life Center North Foursquare Church was planted in 1999 as a small group from Life Center. After meeting in homes for a few months, God opened up the door for us to meet at Northwood Middle School and 500 people showed up on our first Sunday. God has been awesome, stretching us and growing us into what is now a church of over 1200 people meeting in four services. It is obvious to all of us that we are a part of something bigger than ourselves and the Holy Spirit is at work. Literally hundreds of people have come into a relationship with Jesus Christ, been baptized and are now following the Savior. Our church is called to play an important part in restoring broken lives. In 2005 we started Serve Spokane, a non-profit organization whose mission is to serve and love hurting people throughout Spokane with food, clothing, shelter, addiction recovery and support for people with special needs. Life Center North has a huge heart for the global harvest; we are supporting church planters, building wells, fighting malaria, and planting churches in Africa, Nepal, and other countries. We have always been a train and equip kind of church: we founded the Spokane Ministry Institute where we disciple believers, develop leaders, raise up pastors and help plant churches. We have seen graduates of our program launch churches inter-denominationally. Both Serve Spokane and Spokane Ministry Institute are city wide and inter-denominational in their approach. God has called us as a resource church to build up the body of Christ in Spokane and around the world. Recently we launched Catalyst, a credentialed Bible training program for 18-24 year olds which is an immersion discipleship residential program. Life Center North is a spiritually passionate environment made up of people from all walks of life who come together to get real, experience God, have fun, and be changed more and more into the image of Jesus Christ.

"For the past 8 years we have been leasing an old theatre and this has worked great for us. The owner has terminated our lease and he will be demolishing the building in order to develop his land. We have one year to relocate yet we know God is in control. We want to continue reaching out to the hurting world around us with the good news of Jesus Christ. So with that in mind, we began the capital campaign to raise funds to purchase a facility. At the same time, doors opened and doors closed as God clearly pointed the way to the Division Street property. Our goal of $2 million was not raised, but what we did raise will provide an operating facility sufficient for our current needs."

Liferoads: "Life Center Foursquare Church began planting daughter churches in Spokane County in 1997. In the fall of 2000, Joe Wittwer, the pastor of Life Center, contacted Brad and Cheri Williams in Phoenix, Arizona, regarding the possibility of planting a church in Spokane. After ten months of prayer and consideration, the Williams family moved to Spokane. Brad participated for twelve months on the staff at Life Center working in singles ministry and as one of the teaching pastors.

"In late spring of 2002, the birth of a new daughter church was announced, and the development of the Liferoads core team began. Liferoads Church officially began in September of 2002. For the first eight months, Liferoads met in the gym of Longfellow Elementary School. "After those grueling months of being a portable church, setting up and tearing down each week, God provided a phenomenal facility, the former Eastside Cinema. Seating over four hundred with rooms for children's and adult classes, this building has been an amazing blessing from the spring of 2003 to the present.

"In the summer of 2005, Brad and Cheri Williams accepted a call to move to New York City to begin a work planting churches in the city. Grant Opland became the pastor in August 2005 and served wholeheartedly until God called him to other things in January 2009. Grant – along with his wife and kids – were a part of the core team of people who helped start Liferoads. His son Matthew has been the worship pastor since the beginning of Liferoads and he continues to serve today at Liferoads with his wife, Kristin.

"In February of 2009, Donnie Johnson became the pastor of Liferoads Church. Donnie and his wife, Pam, were also a part of the core team that founded Liferoads in 2002. Formerly, Donnie spent two years as the children's pastor and two years as the associate pastor at Liferoads as well as 18 months as the associate pastor at Liferoads' sister church, Mirabeau Chapel in Spokane Valley."

Mosaic Fellowship: "The church hopes to reach the 18 to 35 age group. 'They seem to be leaving and staying away from church in droves,' said Rev. John Repsold, start-up pastor for Mosaic Fellowship. The unusual venue may be a big draw.

The church meets on Sunday mornings at Interplayers Theatre."

"The name chosen for this new congregation has special meaning. A mosaic is a work of art made from small bits of ceramic or glass. Repsold said that's what they're all about. 'The idea of brokenness, of broken pieces of different colors, being put together by a master artist to make something beautiful.'" Their Web site stated "We're located downtown because we want to experience the heart of God in the heart of our city - where we live, work and play in Spokane."

"At Mosaic we try to connect people together in relationships that allow various groups to enjoy each other's friendship while connecting us together as a multi-generational family. Twice a month (one Saturday afternoon and the third Friday evening of the month) Mosaic's young adults gather in different family homes or meet at Second Space Gallery to experience serving some segment of our city together."

Summit Ridge: "One could say that the new Summit Ridge Foursquare Church is opening its doors this weekend, if it had any doors to call its own. "Instead, the new church will meet for now in the Seventh-day Adventist Church at 5607 S. Freya. "While a lot of work remains for Summit Ridge, including finding a permanent site, the church is starting with 300 members and several programs for adults and kids.

"Summit Ridge was formed by Life Center, a church with more than 2,000 members on the North Side. The Rev. Joe Woodruff, hired by Life Center last fall to get the new church up and running, will be pastor. "This is Woodruff's third church planting, and he said it is a ministry he enjoys. A church planting, sometimes called birthing a new church, occurs when some members of a church branch off and form a new church to serve a different area.

"Church planting is the most effective way of reaching people and meeting their needs, said Woodruff, and it allows him to plan the church according to the needs of the community and build it from the ground up. 'I spent three months just getting a sense of the community,' he said. He began by forming Kids Universe, a children's ministry. It includes a church for kids with puppets and animated storytelling. He also plans a tutoring program during the week. It eventually will be expanded to offer children help in numerous subjects from drama to computers. 'The possibilities are endless,' said Woodruff. He's also planning a women's ministry and a music program.

"Woodruff, 34, got his start in ministry at age 16 when he was invited to speak at a youth service. As a result, his older brother was converted to Christianity, and Woodruff decided to make preaching his future. 'For me, preaching and pastoring has been my opportunity to make a difference,' he said." They are still renting that facility.

Final Thoughts

Under the title "There is more than one right way to do church!" Justin Bryeans visited three Mega-Churches for LDR--"Leadership Development Resources LLC." LDR was formed out of a commitment to a biblically-based, Christ-centered mission to develop leaders and empower churches. Of the three churches Bryeans visited, two were in Post Falls, Idaho, and the third was Life Center in Spokane. Here is what he wrote "This Four Square church uses the seven-day-a-week (Christian Center) approach. . . It has very full programming throughout the week with something for everyone. The service was contemporary traditional with a great deal of production and media. It was not a simple church style. They were also working through a book of the Bible in their messages for the summer."

Organic is a word that kept coming up when discussing the Life Center young adult programs. If something isn't working, they change it. They don't seem to have any formal survey data, program evaluation, or focus groups; they just pray a lot and let the Spirit guide them.

They accept people where they are. They don't try to change them. Relationship is a key component to the success of the church and relationship can only come through interaction. Peer leadership is important. Sometimes the college-age students volunteer. Other times church leaders seek out individuals they see with leadership potential and then empower them and train them to lead.

The key findings from Life Center Foursquare Church and its young adult ministry might be summarized as follows:

Food: They have found this to be an important factor as it creates an easy atmosphere for students to get their other student friends to come to a function.

Music: Most young people want uplifting, powerful, and positive contemporary music to listen to and sing along with, and a full band to energize.

Bible-based: People, especially young people, prefer speakers to share the Bible in stories and in ways that they can apply to their life. Application is key. If they don't know what it has to do with them, they won't know how to adapt it to their life.

Involvement: Everyone likes to be involved. With different temperaments, there would be different types of involvement. Ministries can empower young people to help, beginning where they are comfortable. Having a part in something enables people to feel included, not just a spectator.

The Arts: This successful ministry embraces the arts. Videos, photography, art, drama, and other arts are included in their programming.

Connection: They use Twitter, Facebook, etc., to keep in touch with the young people in ways that are comfortable to them.

Acceptance: Successful ministries embrace Matthew 7:1 "Do not judge." They encourage others in their walk with the Lord wherever that may be and seek not to be a stumbling block for them.

Love them: This age group faces many challenges of schedules, relationships, career decisions, and more. They just want to know someone genuinely cares.

Life Center credits a lot of their success to their Life Groups, which are small groups that any size church can emulate.

Tamara Michalenko Terry is a freelance writer with a passion to see young people involved in church ministries and excited about something greater than themselves. She has a degree in public relations and broadcast journalism and has written for a variety of clients for the past 20 years.

References

ALIVE Web site: http://www.lifecenter.net/connect/adults/alive-age-18-25/

Bryeans, Justin (2010). "There is more than one right way to do church!," Leadership Development Resources LLC. http://www.ldrteam.com/2010/08/31/there-is-more-than-one-right-way-to-do-church/

College Housing web site: http://www.lifecenter.net/connect/adults/alive-age-18-25/college-housing/

Culver, Nina (1997). "Church Opens at Temporary Site," *The Spokesman-Review*, September 18, 1997, http://www.spokesman.com/stories/1997/sep/18/church-opens-at-temporary-site/

De Leon, Virginia (2005). "Church's size can't hinder welcome," *The Spokesman-Review*, December 12, 2005. www.spokesman.com/stories/2005/dec/12/churchs-size-cant-hinder-welcome/

Eastpoint web site: http://eastpointchurch.org/im/history/

Foursquare Church history: www.foursquare.org/about/history/

Gallup Poll (2012). "Confidence in organized religion hits all-time low in Gallup poll" http://usnews.msnbc.msn.com/_news/2012/07/12/12706531-confidence-in-organized-religion-hits-all-time-low-in-gallup-poll?lite

Life Center Church web site: www.lifecenter.net/new-here/

Life Center North web site: http://faithvisionsacrifice.org/our-story

Liferoads web site: http://www.liferoads.org/history.html

McBride, Kelly (1995a). "Crowds Challenge Church," *The Spokesman-Review*, November 12, 1995. http://www.spokesman.com/stories/1995/nov/12/crowds-challenge-church/

McBride, Kelly (1995b). "And A Multitude Gathered Growth Spurt Hurtles Congregations Into World Of Mega-Churches," *The Spokesman-Review*, November 12, 1995. www.spokesman.com/stories/1995/nov/12/and-a-multitude-gathered-growth-spurt-hurtles/

Morlin, Bill (2006). "Easter brings supersized services for some," *The Spokesman-Review*, April 17, 2006. www.spokesman.com/stories/2006/apr/17/easter-brings-supersized-services-for-some/

Mosaic web site: http://www.mosaicspokane.com/

Neely, Jamie Tobias (1996). "5,200 Attend Easter Services At Arena Music, Spotlights, Videos Create Rock Concert Atmosphere At Celebration," *The Spokesman-Review*, April 8, 1996. http://www.spokesman.com/stories/1996/apr/08/5200-attend-easter-services-at-arena-music/

Soul Punch Video web site: http://www.lifecenter.net/connect/adults/alive-age-18-25/soulpunch-videos/

Spokane, Washington, statistics: www.city-data.com/city/Spokane-Washington.html

Summit Ridge web site: http://www.srcf.org/

Chapter 8
New Life Covenant Church
Chicago, Illinois

By Donna Lee Granville

New Life Covenant Church (NLC) was founded in September of 2003 under the leadership of Pastor John F. Hannah. Beginning only with weekly Bible studies and a small committed group of followers, in less than a year NLC began holding weekly Sunday services as their numbers grew quickly. Just four short years later, in October of 2008, NLC's rapid growth led to the purchasing of its first building, The Tabernacle, located in the Grand Crossing neighborhood, a predominantly African American middle class neighborhood on Chicago's Southside. However, that move was short-lived as New Life soon outgrew its facilities and began holding two services at 10 am and 1pm at the University of Illinois-Chicago forum at the intersection of Roosevelt and Halsted streets. Now in 2012, NLC has once again outgrown its facilities with the 3,000 person capacity of UIC forum being met and exceeded at both services nearly every Sunday. In fact, for special services such as Easter Sunday and New Year's, New Life holds its services at Chicago State University solely to accommodate its membership.

To meet its need for new facilities, NLC has, at this writing, purchased land and begun the process of building a new church campus. However, in the meantime, NLC is considering adding additional Sunday services, bringing its total to four meeting times in two different locations. NLC's exponential growth is such that despite its relatively young age, it is already being considered a mega church in the city of Chicago. In addition, New Life streams its Sunday services, Bible study and twice-monthly prayer meetings online, further broadening the scope and reach of its ministry. While NLC does not specifically endorse a denomination, its parent church, also called New Life Covenant, is affiliated with the Assemblies of God denomination, whose four-fold mission is to "evangelize the lost, worship God, disciple believers, and show compassion." (Assemblies of God website)

A typical Sunday at New Life Covenant includes three services held at two different locations: an 8 a.m. service at the Tabernacle, and 10 a.m. and 1 p.m. services at the UIC forum. Services at NLC typically last between an hour-and-a-half to two hours, with very few times when a service goes over the two-hour mark. At the services held at the UIC forum, seating is almost always at capacity, with ushers serving the necessary role of aiding congregants in finding seating in the main hall and if necessary in the overflow rooms. Similarly, weekly Thursday night Bible studies and twice monthly Tuesday morning prayer meetings also adhere to the one-and-a-half to two-hour time frame. Though NLC's vision is to be a multicultural ministry, its congregation is overwhelmingly Black/African American with a small percentage of members of other racial/ethnic backgrounds. Consequently, services take place in English and as yet there are no accommodations for the deaf or hearing-impaired. However, the congregation is diverse in other ways, with various arrangements of couples, families and friends, the young, the old and the in-between.

Over the course of New Life Covenant's nine-year existence, a characterizing feature of its ministry has been its rapid growth. This growth has often been surprising for both insiders and outsiders. Pastor Hannah has told the story of other pastors whose reaction to NLC's rapid increase in numbers has been to say "it will slow down soon." Yet, NLC's numbers show no signs of slowing down.

A very visible and important demographic group in NLC's growing numbers is the youth and young adult population. In place of statistical information from the specific ministries that cater to this population within New Life Covenant, estimates of the size of this population are drawn from observations of Sunday services. For example, NLC potentially adds many new members to its congregation through the altar call which takes place at the end of each service. While the number of people who respond to the altar call fluctuates from service to service and can range in number from 40 to over a 100 people, 18- to 29-year-olds often make up half if not more of the new additions to NLC. Some of these may be new believers who will become new members.

Similarly, in a typical New Life Sunday service the youth and young adult population, though perhaps not quite at the 50% mark, is very visible and seems to comprise between 25-35% of those in attendance. Furthermore, if altar calls are any indication, the 18- to 29-year-old population is drawn to the way in which New Life Covenant presents the gospel of Christ. New Life's numbers are impressive in light of research that indicates African-American youth and young adults under the age of 30 are less likely to be religiously affiliated in comparison to African-Americans age 50 and older. (Saghal and Smith)

How, then, is NLC able to successfully recruit, retain, and engage the African -American youth and young adult population? While there is no one factor that has solely determined NLC's success with youth, there does seem to be an overarching philosophy of action that directly impacts the way in which youth and young adults receive NLC and the programs and activities that NLC designates for this particular group. According to the NLC website, its vision is to be, "A multicultural, family-oriented and cutting-edge ministry known by its dynamic worship, excellence in management and operations, Christ-like character of its members and life-changing compassion for people of all backgrounds." (NLC website) An important part of this vision is the goal of showing "life changing compassion" regardless of background, to all who enter New Life's doors.

 Those sentiments are echoed by Pastor Hannah in an interview done in September of 2010. When discussing the rapid growth experienced by New life Covenant, Pastor Hannah asserts that "I love God and I love his people, sheep

163

are not stupid—they know when people care about them."
(Rolfe 2010) In that same interview Pastor Hannah makes it
plain that New Life Covenant is a church that sees itself as
ministering specifically to the unsaved and the unchurched.
According to Pastor Hannah, "Churches swap members ... but
I tell my members don't bring me your cousin that's saved, but
bring me your unsaved cousin or aunt—we want the ones that
don't go to church...bring me the ones that are lost." (Rolfe
2010) Bringing in the unchurched is accomplished through
New Life's outreach efforts that take place primarily in the
Grand Crossing neighborhood where the Tabernacle is
located. These outreach events include activities such as a
back-to-school carnival or cleaning up and praying for the
neighborhood.

The focus on showing compassion and relating to all people
regardless of background and the emphasis on recruiting the
unchurched in particular are important factors that seem to
underlie all of NLC's programming and activities for youth and
young adults. Often for this demographic group, church itself
holds little to no relevance to the day-to-day lives they lead.
However, at NLC there are more than a few examples within
the programming and activities for youth and young adults that
represent attempts to meet the needs of this group on a
holistic level, not just spiritually.

One of the most visible manifestations of this is the way in
which Sunday services are structured to be engaging through
the incorporation of elements such as music and the use of
the arts and drama. A typical Sunday morning worship
service at NLC begins with the praise and worship team and
band that play a mix of different musical styles including
contemporary Christian rock, gospel and hip hop songs. Much
like a concert, the mood is set with dimmed overhead lights,
special strobe lights on the stage, and an area cleared directly
in front of the stage for members to dance and sing along to
the praise and worship portion of the service. In addition to
the praise and worship team, the NLC dance team also
occupies a place on the stage with a team of approximately 10

to 20 dancers accompanying the singers and musicians. Dance and music are not the only arts used during Sunday services. Often Pastor Hannah's sermons themselves are presented not only in words through his preaching but also through other visual aids. Some examples include the use of spoken word in conveying a message on sexual purity and the use of dramatic vignettes to convey a message about the perils of surrounding oneself with the wrong people. Technology also plays an important role as scriptures are displayed on wide-screen projectors and even announcements are done in the style of commercials complete with NLC television correspondents.

Along with the music, worship style, and the integration of the arts and technology, NLC is also attractive to youth and young adults because of its extremely charismatic founding pastor, John F. Hannah. As already mentioned, Pastor Hannah's sermons are often dynamic in nature because of the emphasis placed on providing visual aids that bring to life his words and scriptures in real, relevant, and relational ways. In addition, Pastor Hannah shares personal anecdotes and stories that highlight the ways in which his personal relationship with God has not only matured over time but also influences how he lives his life daily. Stories from the pulpit have included candid remarks about smoking marijuana, and even about fights and growing pains with his wife of 18 years. Through it all, Pastor Hannah manages to convey his message with a mixture of wit, humor, and refreshing honesty. Perhaps due to hosting his own morning radio show, he is also very in tune to pop culture and can casually refer to rappers or songs of the moment, familiar to his hearers. According to Pastor Hannah, "People told me that God would never use me because I am too silly. So I walked around trying to be serious. God has used me and my comedy to use and reach people. God has his hands on my life and has chosen me to preach for this generation." (Rolfe 2010) Perhaps Pastor Hannah is indeed right, because as a charismatic leader, he is an initial, if not primary, reason why youth and young adults, along with others regardless of their station in life, become attracted to New Life Covenant Church.

While the setup of services and the charisma of the senior pastor may initially aid in the recruitment of youth and young adults, what is that keeps them coming back for more? NLC attempts to meet that goal by offering a number of programs and ministries that specifically cater to the youth and young adult population. For youth ranging in age from early teens to late teens, the Identity teen ministry offers a number of programs designed to meet their specific needs. These programs range from those which cater to spiritual needs, such as classes on purity and the foundations of a Christian walk, to programs like the step team, dance, and praise teams that cater to other needs.

In addition to the various programs housed under the Identity ministry, each Friday a youth church service is held that promises to convey the gospel "in a fun, radical, real yet motivating way." (NLC website) The full list of programs and activities housed under the Identity umbrella consists of the following: weekly Friday youth service, foundational class, purity class, identity athletics, a team of young prayer warriors that intercede for themselves and others, helping support teens throughout high school and preparing them for life after high school, Young Ladies of Light specifically for teen girls, Boyz 2 Men specifically for teen boys, the Pursue program that keeps track of teens to help provide support as necessary, Step team, Praise team, Spoken word/rap/DJ teams, and the 4HisGlory Human Video team.

For young adults who are above the age of 18, their participation in New Life Covenant Church is a bit harder to untangle as there are multiple programs with considerable overlap and as a result they share this population. The programs that cater to young adults include the Singles Power of 1 ministry that aims to teach singles to develop an intimate one-on-one relationship with God; principles for Christian dating and tips for marriage preparation; the Love Sister 2

166

Sister ministry that provides support and encouragement for women regardless of age or position in life; the Iron Sharpens Iron men's ministry that ministers to men regardless of age; and the New Life Connect Three College support group for students enrolled at all levels of higher education.

Thus, for older young adults the programming and activities offered at New Life are specific to the particular needs of that young adult. For example, a 25-year-old graduate student might find the Singles Power of 1 ministry more suitable than the college support group. In a similar vein, a 29-year-old working male might find more of his needs met by the Iron Sharpens Iron ministry, and for those who are married, the One Flesh marriage ministry might be more fitting than others. These programs provide this age group with multiple choices to determine which programs and activities might be most beneficial to their lives.

Along with the monthly fellowships held by each individual ministry, there are also many opportunities for those interested to serve on various committees that deal with the arts and drama, publicity and media, or outreach and service projects. Activities such as Prayer on the Nine and Clean the Green invite youth and young adults to take active service roles in the community. These activities are designed to show that life within a Christian context does not have to lack excitement or always be religious in nature. For example, for Valentine's Day, the Power of 1 Singles ministry hosted its own event at a hotel in the city, complete with secular music and a DJ.

In summary, there are a multitude of ways in which New Life Covenant provides youth and young adults with opportunities to get exactly what they need according to their particular position or station in life.

Why Is This Ministry Effective?

NLC seems to be successful in recruiting, retaining, and engaging their youth and young adults for three key reasons.

First, their philosophy of action is one that focuses on bringing in the unchurched and showing them "life-changing compassion" regardless of their backgrounds. NLC's various outreach and service projects are manifestations of its goal to go after the lost and introduce them to Christ. While this focus is perhaps in many ways not particularly unique, it might be especially successful with the youth and young adult population who often see churches and their congregations as places for judgment and chastisement rather than compassion.

Second, the charismatic leadership of Pastor Hannah attracts youth and young adults due to his ability to relate personally though preaching to an audience of thousands. Pastor Hannah's honesty about his own experiences along his Christian walk and his willingness to share moments of failure and succumbing to temptation add to his likeability and ability to relate to youth and young adults. In addition, his sermons are engaging and dynamic and his use of use visual aids ensure that his message, whether it be on sexual purity or lessons from the life of David, is driven home and made relevant for his congregants' day-to-day lives.

Third, NLC offers a wide array of diverse programs, activities, and ministries for youth and young adults that provide this population with opportunities to get what they need spiritually and in other ways as well. In their 2005 book, *The Hip Hop Church*, authors Smith and Jackson contend that, "in some ways youth and young adults can feel like second-class citizens in the church, sitting in the back of the church while the adults 'get their praise on.' ... When youth are recognized, it is because they are serving in the youth choir, youth usher board, or youth council---merely mimicking adults and their behavior in the church." (Smith & Jackson 2005:41) Where NLC attempts to prevent this from happening is by offering the youth and young adult population with tailored choices that allow them to determine how they will participate according to their own position in life.

Today, churches in general and perhaps largely black churches in particular, can no longer take for granted the role they have historically played in the lives of families and youth and young adults. There is a growing number of unchurched and unsaved individuals even within the historically religious African-American community. How churches respond to this population, especially youth and young adults, will determine the role of church and religion at large in generations to come.

Despite claims that many young people within the United States are largely alienated from religion, within the African-American community religion still remains an important authority in the lives of youth and young adults. Research on adolescents' participation finds that in comparison to other racial groups, African-American adolescents attend church more regularly, pray more regularly, are more likely to be a part of a church youth group, and claim religion to be a very important part of their lives. (Smith et al. 2002) Among the under 30 crowd, an overwhelming 81% of those who claim affiliation with historically black Protestant churches maintain that religion is an important factor in their lives. (Pond, Smith & Clement 2010)

However, this is changing. Research on the millennial generation (those born after the year 1980) suggests a growing generational gap as young adults attend church services less frequently, are less likely to name religion as an important factor in their lives when compared to their elders (Pond, Smith & Clement 2010). Among African-Americans under age 30, 19% report being unaffiliated with religion in comparison to just 7% of African Americans aged 50 and older. (Saghal & Smith 2008)

These statistics raise important concerns about the future of the black church and its influence on youth and young adults. While the level of religious involvement for African-American youth and young adults remains high, there is a growing generational divide between youth and older generations. In the article "Inner-city Black Churches Struggle to Blend Youth,

Tradition," journalist David Briggs follows one inner-city Cleveland congregation in its attempt to close the generational gap in part by relaxing dress codes, incorporating technology, and tweaking music style. "What gives the issue of music a special urgency, church observers say, is that one can no longer count on succeeding generations to come through church doors." (Briggs 2008) NLC has seemingly taken notice and follows suit in its relaxed dress codes, music and worship style and use of technology.

In their seminal work, *The Black Church in the African American Experience*, Lincoln and Mamiya (1990) find that the primary reasons most youth and young adults leave the black church are due to a lack of relevant church programs and the absence of meaningful ways for youth to engage in church activities. (Lincoln & Mamiya 327) Thus, NLC's focus on offering programming and activities for the youth and young adult population to be engaged is an important approach to ensuring the continued relevancy of church for a seemingly disengaged or disengaging generation.

However, most important of the aforementioned three reasons is the focus on bringing in new people and showing them compassion. The idea that the black (or any) church can no longer count on generations of families to come through the doors is important when considering the future of the church. Youth and young adults are an important demographic for membership continuity as they in turn grow up and raise families in and through the church. Consequently, for churches, mosques, synagogues and other religious institutions to survive, they must concern themselves with ensuring that younger generations continue to see the relevance of religious participation and involvement in their lives. NLC is but one example of a church that is willing to find the seekers, the unchurched, and the lost among the youth and young adult population, to bring them into the fold under the leadership of compassionate shepherds, and to provide them with opportunities to see the relevance and benefits of Christianity and church participation in their lived experiences.

170

Donna Lee Granville is a Ph.D. candidate at the University of Illinois-Chicago. Her dissertation will examine the intersections of religious participation, generation and racial identity in the perceptions of belonging among West Indian and African immigrants. Her research interests include race and ethnicity, immigration (specifically Black immigrants), religion and cultural studies. She was born and raised on the island of Jamaica, moving to Brooklyn at the age of 10. She considers her experience growing up in a vibrant Caribbean community in New York City to be an important influence on her research.

References

Briggs, David (2008). "Inner-City Black Churches Struggle to Blend Youth, Tradition,"
Cleveland.com.
www.cleveland.com/religion/index.ssf/2008/12/innercity_black_churches_strug.html

Identity Teen Ministry:
www.youtube.com/watch?v=Mi7fJQmmyhE&feature=related

Identity Teen Ministry Spoken word:
www.youtube.com/watch?v=J8S_KmQQubl&feature=relmfu

Identity Teen Ministry Praise and Worship Team:
www.youtube.com/watch?v=kkZmHkQ_018&feature=relmfu

Lincoln, C. Eric, and Lawrence H. Mamiya (1990). *The Black Church and the African American Experience*. Durham, NC: Duke University Press.

New Life Covenant Church web site: www.newlifeoakwood.org

Pond, Allision, Gregory Smith and Scott Clement (2010). "Religion Among the Millennials." Pew Forum.
www.pewforum.org/Age/Religion

Rolfe, Effie (2010). "Rev. John Hannah handles growing flock at New Life   Covenant," *The Chicago Defender*.
http://www.chicagodefender.com/article-8921-rev-john-hannah-handles-growing-flock-at-new-life-covenant.html

Saghal, Neha and Greg Smith (2009). "A Religious Portrait of African-Americans." Pew Forum. www.pewforum.org/A-Religious-Portrait-of-African-Americans.aspx

Smith, Efrem and Phil Jackson (2005). *The Hip-hop Church: Connecting With the Movement Shaping Our Culture*. Downers Grove, IL: InterVarsity Press.

Smith, Christian, Melinda Denton, Robert Faris and Mark Regenerus (2002). "Mapping American Adolescent Religious Participation," *Journal for the Scientific Study of Religion* 41 (4): 597-612.

Chapter 9
Old Saint Patrick's Church
Chicago, Illinois

By Courtney Ann Irby

This case study profiles Old St. Patrick's Church, a Catholic congregation located at 700 West Adams Street, Chicago, Illinois 60661. The extensive clergy team of Old St. Pat's, as the church is commonly known, is led by Father Thomas J. Hurley. Keara Ette is responsible for the young adult ministry but the historical commitment to reaching out to young adults has meant that much of the staff contributes to these efforts.

In reflecting on the needs and desires of laity, the church strives to be a place of hospitality, great music, and inspired teaching. As their website explains, "Nothing is more important to the mission of Old St. Patrick's Church than the hospitality extended to each person who crosses our threshold, whether as a first-time visitor or as a member of the Old St. Pat's community." They live out this commitment by having a time early in the services to greet and introduce themselves to other attendees. The rest of the service is full of liturgical Catholic hymns that are elevated by the beautiful voices of the choir and preaching that seeks to contextualize biblical teachings with contemporary concerns to provide thought-provoking homilies.

Key Data

Old St. Pat's is a large urban congregation with approximately 3,500 registered households that come from about 200 zip codes within the greater Chicago area. In order to serve this large membership they regularly offer six services on Sundays. Those who like to attend church early can choose from a 7:00 am or 8:00 am service, while those who prefer a more leisurely Sunday morning can choose from a 9:30 am, 11:15 am or 12:45 pm service. Finally, those who prefer an evening service can attend 5:00 pm services or, during the summer, a sunset service at 8:00 pm. The 5:00 pm service is popular for young adults, in part due to the time but also because throughout the year they offer programming for the young adults after this service. In addition to Sunday services, the congregation also offers services Monday through Friday at 7:00 am and 12:00 pm. All the services are offered in English.

The programming is fairly evenly split between staff and lay young adults. While initially the young adult ministers did the vast majority of the administrative, brainstorming, planning and execution of events/activities, that has changed over the years. With the success of their programming, their intentional efforts to include young adults in leadership (including hiring young adults as staff members and encouraging them to serve on committees outside of YA ministries) and their ability to build up lay leadership over the years, the events are now more coordinated and designed by lay, young adults. Ette estimates that the distribution is about 50 to 60 percent member driven and 40 percent staff driven. Specifically, the staff continues to be responsible for all the administrative and financial side of planning events. Budget and bills remain under the staff's responsibilities, but the design and coordination of young adult programs has shifted to be more run by the young adults. For instance, the evening prayer rituals (peer-ministry) was initially developed by staff but is now run by young adults for other young adults.

While the Mass on Sundays represents a significant source of involvement in the community, it is far from the only way that people participate in the community of Old St. Pat's. In addition to their weekly services, they offer a wide array of programming. Whether it is for families, teens, young adults, or adults the parish offers a variety of ministries, lecture series, volunteer opportunities and events. Finally, a key way that people become acquainted with and potentially involved in the church is through the sacraments. For instance, Old St. Pat's hosts approximately 150 weddings a year and, as will be discussed later, each wedding involves a marriage preparation at the church.

Perhaps due to all of these activities or because of the quality of the services, the church continues to grow. Eleven months out of the year they hold a new members' dinner that includes 20 to 40 new additions to the church on average. In other words, between 220 and 440 new people join Old St. Pat's each year. Of course, as Fr. Hurley pointed out, this does not always indicate a net gain of this many new people to the church roster annually because their high percentage of young adults and urban professionals means their population is highly transitory. Specifically, they estimate that 40 percent of their registered members are young adults, however, these numbers do indicate the strength and overall growth of the church.

Demographics and Culture

As is evident by the name, Old St. Patrick's Church is a historically Irish congregation. While the demographics of the church have shifted away from these Irish roots, the church building maintains a distinctly Irish feel. Stepping inside to face the altar, one sees a large statue of Old St. Patrick holding a handful of clovers, and walls covered with intricate paintings of Book of Kells-inspired Celtic knots. Despite the markers of Irish heritage in the church's appearance, the services and church community lack a strong sense of ethnic Irish culture. In fact, what is striking looking around the full pews is the relative diversity of the congregation. While the congregation remains predominately white, there is a notable presence of racial/ethnic minorities that gather to worship.

Central to the identity and culture of Old St. Pat's is its location in Chicago's West Loop. This location is adjacent to downtown but also immediately off the main highways that connect the city to the suburbs (I-90/I-94 and I-290). Additionally, it is conveniently located on local transit lines and close to the train station in downtown Chicago. Due to the location, attendees can easily commute from not only the nearby west side of Chicago but from all over the city, suburbs, and even northern Indiana. The free parking and many empty lots on Sundays makes driving downtown to attend church potentially more convenient than some of the parishes in other Chicago neighborhoods. As a result, compared to many Catholic parishes that continue to operate as neighborhood churches, Old St. Pat's has cultivated itself into a commuter parish.

While this commuter culture is predominantly an artifact of their spatial location in the city, they have also embraced this identity. In fact, they draw on their Irish heritage to theologically understand themselves as a church "meeting at the crossroads" symbolized by the Celtic cross that adorns the walls of the church. In his religious artwork for the church, Thomas O'Shaughnessy included the Celtic cross, which is an encircled cross, as a central motif in both the painting and stained glass. Elfriede Wedam, a sociologist who studied the parish in the 1990s, explains that historically this symbol was used on ancient city maps to represent the walls protecting city residents but that Old St. Pat's "has reinterpreted and used this symbolism to connect the church with the city as a whole, reaching beyond traditional parish boundaries" (221). The combination of viewing all of greater Chicago as their "parish" and their emphasis on hospitality has meant that they are intentional about creating events for new members to the community and offering a wide variety of programming to target various populations.

Background and History

As one of the few buildings to survive the Chicago Fire of 1871, Old St. Pat's represents a Chicago institution. As former Mayor Richard M. Daley explained in a book commissioned to commemorate the 150th anniversary of the church, "People throughout Chicago recognize Old Saint Pat's as the historical center of the Irish community, but its story is not simply the story of one church in one community serving one ethnic group. It is the story of communities throughout our city." (ix).

As the oldest church building and second oldest parish in the city, the history of Old St. Pat's congregation reflects the historical trends of Chicago.

Established in 1846, the church initially served the Irish immigrant population until the mid-twentieth century, when changes to the city threatened the parish. The church was first threatened with demolition in 1950 because of the construction of the expressways. While it survived this threat, the neighborhood around it did not. Between displacement due to the expressway cutting the neighborhood in half and the general process of people increasingly leaving the city for the suburbs, the surrounding neighborhood became predominantly an industrial area which would a few decades later experience its own decline. By the 1980s the congregation had shrunk to only four registered members. It was at this time that Father John J. Wall stepped in and began a process of revitalization.

Fr. Wall approached the parish with a new vision. In looking out at the neighborhood he saw potential in what had previously been barriers to growth. Specifically, he believed that the expressway that had once helped to decimate their population and isolate the church now could serve as a way to rejuvenate the community. The revitalization of downtown, which included the new construction of buildings on the West Side like the Sears Tower, meant that thousands of cars were regularly brought to the church's front door. A key part of Fr. Wall's redevelopment plan involved creating a metropolitan church that would serve young adults and minister to urban professionals. Refusing to believe in the life-cycle theory that said young adults drift away from the church, he sought ways to target and serve young adult populations by tapping into preexisting groups, such as encouraging the Young Irish Fellowship Club to use their facilities. In what he called an "Inside-Out Church," Fr. Wall redesigned the congregation around the idea that the church must seek to understand and respond to the world. Rather than assume people would come to the church on their own and find ways to fit the needs of the church into their own lives, he sought to find ways that the church could serve laity and be meaningful in their lives.

These efforts were resoundingly successful because by the late-1990s the church had 2,800 registered members, most of whom were drawn from the greater Chicago area. Also, through their own fundraising efforts they were able to complete a multimillion-dollar restoration of the architectural and artistic features of the historic church building. Under the present leadership of Fr. Thomas Hurley, the church continues to understand young adults as central to their ministry but recognizes that many of those young adults that first helped to expand the church under Fr. Wall's tenure have now become adults with their own children. The church now prides itself on being a multigenerational church that tries to serve the needs of each generation individually, while also considering the multiple generations of the community as the collective body of the church.

Underlying Philosophy

For decades, the mission statement of Old St. Pat's has been "Serving the life and the work of the laity in the world." The vision behind this mission statement was that Old St. Pat's was a faith community that would help to serve and build up the laity in order for the laity to go and serve the world. While currently they are in the midst of a period of self-reflection on this mission statement, it still represents an underlying philosophy of their approach to laity broadly, and to the life situation of young adults particularly. As sociologist Elfriede Wedam notes, "the kind of participation Old Saint Pat's asks of its members respects the broad pluralism of everyday life; at the same time, it refuses to build a church simply around their needs" (217). Her observation can be seen in some of the ways that they conceptualize the concept of "church."

According to the church website, "The people who gather at Old St. Patrick's are building an experience called church: (1) that stands squarely at the intersection of faith and life; (2) that rests on a foundation of welcome and hospitality; (3) whose walls define a sanctuary for the growth of intimacy with God and a deepening of relationships with others; (4) that is richly textured by the diversity of peoples and generations; (5) whose cornerstone is hewn from a commitment to compassionate service and justice; (6) that is illumined by the Light of Christ; (7) whose roof is frequently raised by the joyous celebrations of life; and (8) whose doors and windows are always open to the movement of Spirit in the world."

In every iteration of their philosophy, there is an underlying theme of recognizing that churches should not assume the laity exist to serve the church. Rather, they understand church as a collective project and for it to succeed churches must be aware of the needs and life positions of laity. In the case of young adults, this has meant they avoid approaching their ministry from the perspective of "Why don't young adults attend church?" Instead, they ask "How can we reach out to young adults to where they are in life and can we show them that church is meaningful when they reach out to us?"

Outreach with Young Adults

One of the key ways that Old St. Pat's has reached out to young adults is by seeking to integrate church into relevant areas of their lives and intentionally seeking to build relationships when young adults reach out to the church. Consistent with their concept of being a church that serves the laity, Old St. Pat's has constructed four main types of ministry centered around learning, spirituality, service and community, all of which are part of larger effort to missionize to young adults. While these ministries are open to other age groups, they represent intentional programming designed for young adults and have emerged out of decades of building relationships with them, asking what they are interested in, and finding out what they need.

Learning – One of the prominent ways that Old St. Pat's ministers to young adults is by hosting a variety of lectures and discussion series. These events are hosted for several weeks during most seasons, which means that there are regular opportunities to attend a learning session at the church. Rather than use these as a way to teach young adults the Catholic catechism, they view learning series as opportunities for young adults to come together to discuss particular aspects of faith and consider how it relates to their lives. One such series is the "Theology on Tap" program which originated at Old St. Pat's but has since spread across Chicago, as well as to over a hundred parishes across the United States and world more broadly. Running for over thirty years now, this series tends to be held during the summer for about four weeks. The series features a group of young adults gathering to drink and discuss relevant matters on theology and religion. In a casual meet-and-greet style the events involve a speaker presenting for approximately a half-hour and then about twenty minutes of discussion and sharing about faith. In the summer of 2013, for instance, the topics focused on cultivating and living out one's spirituality as a young adult.

Spirituality – By providing young adults with opportunities to attend retreats, participate in afternoons of reflection or to lead an evening prayer, Old St. Pat's has oriented another arm of their ministry towards cultivating the spiritual lives of young adults. These spirituality-oriented programs often draw on the young adults' own input and leadership. For instance, the evening prayer program is a type of peer ministry that is a service entirely run and organized by young adults to serve other young adults, as well as other populations. Building off a long tradition within the Catholic community, the church has used the tradition of evening prayers as an opportunity for young adults to be involved in church leadership. Another way that young adults help to plan and structure the events is by suggesting new twists on existing programs or practices. For instance, because some participants enjoyed camping, they instituted camping trips to draw young adults into the practice of spiritual retreats.

Service – Partnering with various organizations around the city, such as shelters or urban Catholic schools, Old St. Pat's organizes a variety of service events throughout the year. For the past twenty years, they have brought groups to volunteer at a local shelter. Seeing that the need for service extends beyond the Chicago area, they have also organized a variety of service trips. For instance, after Hurricane Katrina they took a group of young adults down to help with the cleanup at a parish that they had a connection with in Mississippi. On another trip, they focused on border immersion by taking a group of young adults to the Mexico border on a pilgrimage that sought to reflect on where God is in the difficult situations involving immigration and border disputes. The various service events strive to make the question of "how are we people of faith?" tangible in the lives of their participants. As the young adult minister, Ette, explained, the service aspect has been important for attracting young adults because so many people of this generation want to help and she believes that Old St. Pat's can make this possible by organizing service events.

Community – Especially amongst a transitory demographic, Keara Ette also notes that the church can provide a way to connect and meet people outside of work and the bar scene. As such, the goal of building community among young adults undergirds many of the other types of ministry, as well as serving as a goal in its own right. Much of the young adult programming is scheduled after the 5:00 pm Mass. This allows young adults to participate in the community of the church during the service, and makes the church more inviting as it lives up to its stated goal of hospitality. By periodically creating these times after services to meet and socialize with other young adults, Old St. Pat's can invite them into the church community and allow them to meet other Catholics their own age.

The church also consistently uses various forms of social media to increase community. Every week the church sends out a general email to their members/"friends" (people interested in the church activities but not official members).

This email is not directly aimed at young adults but may include updates about upcoming events. They also send out an email every other week directly to the young adult members/"friends" that details the events, activities, etc. They have a Facebook page that they seek to update daily that includes general happenings at the church which can include YA events. They also have a twitter account with similar postings. Lastly, they have a well-done webpage that provides general information about the church and up-to-date information about different events. The church uses a combination of digital and print media (bulletin, handouts, etc.) to notify people in the greater Chicago area about their events.

These four pillars of their outreach ministry goals do not represent entirely distinct categories of ministry because many of the church's events cross boundaries between the four goals. All four, however, are part of the larger mission of the young adult ministry that emerges from the overall philosophy of Old St. Pat's. The four pillars of their programming represent ways that the church seeks to help young adults engage more deeply in their faith. Recognizing that relationships with God are accomplished through multiple avenues, they seek to construct a varied programming schedule.

The fact that Old St. Pat's is a Chicago institution also helps the outreach of the church. As one young adult who moved to Chicago and began attending Old St. Pat's explained to me, all these programs help to establish a certain level of buzz about the church. Young Catholics in the greater Chicago area all appear to know the name Old St. Pat's even if they have never personally attended. Part of this is due to the notoriety of some its members, such as the former Mayor Daley and his family, but another key factor is their fundraising event, the "World's Largest Block Party," that they have hosted for the past thirty years.

Drawing on the neighborhood practice of blocking off roads and throwing a party, Fr. Wall reclaimed this urban ritual by throwing a street music festival beginning in the 1980s. Especially in the early years, this event would draw large crowds because there were few music festivals in the city. Each year the church closes down the streets in their neighborhood and uses the adjacent parking lots to host various bands, vendors and drinks. In fact the notoriety of this event extends beyond Chicago as evidenced by the description on the Lonely Planet Travel Guide's webpage, "Old St Pat's is best known for its year-round calendar of social events for singles, including the enormously popular World's Largest Block Party; this is a weekend-long party with big-name rock bands where Catholic singles can flirt."

While the above style of programs operates as a type of outreach to young adults by attempting to pull them into church life, Old St. Pat's also offers what Young Adult Minister Ette calls "inreach" programs. These programs involve recognizing and capitalizing on times when young adults approach the church on their own over their life course, and finding ways to make these times meaningful and enjoyable experiences that provide them with a reason to become involved in the church. These inreach programs involve capitalizing on moments such as weddings when young adults often at least briefly establish contact with churches.

Marriage Preparation (Pre-Cana) – Similar to other sacraments in the Catholic Church, members are required to go through a series of classes to learn about the significance of the sacraments and their associated liturgy. In the case of marriage, Catholic dioceses across the country offer a variety of different types of marriage preparation courses to teach couples about the sacraments, and help them look beyond the wedding day and towards the marriage. While the Archdiocese of Chicago offers their own marriage preparation courses, Old St. Pat's decided that rather than have couples getting married at their church attend this diocesan program that could occur at any parish that had opened its doors for that day, they would offer their own Pre-Cana programs.

The decision to commit resources and volunteers to conducting their own marriage preparation emerged from the realization that this represented an opportunity to build relationships with participating couples. By having their own staff organize the event and inviting their own couples who have been married to talk to the participants, they are able to better control the quality of programming and to introduce couples to members of the church. In comparison to the diocesan programming, which includes events with more limited commitment, such as a one-day events, Old St. Pat's always has Pre-Cana occur over a period of three consecutive Sunday afternoons. By conveniently ending the courses at 4:45 pm, they use these classes as a way to also encourage (mostly) young adults to attend the 5:00 pm service with the ministry team. Following their overall philosophy of hospitality, they believe that by offering their own program they can create a more welcoming environment and positive experiences for young couples. They present these efforts as their own investment in couples' marriages by helping to connect them to a faith community that can provide support over their future years as a married couple.

The Rite of Christian Initiative for Adults (RICA) – About forty people a year are brought into the church through the sacraments of initiation, namely baptism, confirmation, and Eucharist. Approximately 80 to 90 percent of these people are young adults who are either converts to Catholicism or were raised Catholic but had not done the sacrament as a child and it was now part of their bucket list. As with the marriage preparation classes, Old St. Pat's has redesigned these courses to fit young adult needs and to help build relationships with them.

Undergirding these efforts remains the philosophy of the church which has sought to serve laity, so that laity can serve and bring God's love into the world. Young adult minister

Keara Ette believes that this mission, especially in how it has been actualized in the above programming, creates a church that is empowering and resonates with young adults. They strive to make church, and by extension religion, not a one-hour experience on Sundays but something that is connected with a community, inviting people to participate in the life of the church in a deeper, more holistic way.

While young adults may find this philosophy empowering, the ones I spoke with felt more inspired by the politics of the church. Situated in a progressive urban city, the few young adults I spoke with resonated with the church's efforts to seriously engage with contemporary issues on which they felt the Church hierarchy has tended to be more conservative. For instance, the church has a gay and lesbian outreach ministry and in 2012 after the Vatican chastised American nuns, they held a prayer service for women religious to honor their good works, kindness and holiness. While Old St. Pat's does not contradict the official teachings of the Church, they have been willing to engage in a discussion on controversial topics which has resonated with young adults. For one young adult, witnessing the congregation's progressive but still distinctly Catholic orientation on contentious issues sends a message to a new generation of Catholics that the church is still relevant.

Young Adults as Both a Subpopulation and the Community

In an attempt to serve but not isolate young adults in the congregation, Old St. Pat's has designed programming to fit the specific spiritual needs of young adults but also seeks to integrate them into the church community as a whole. As Ette explained, the goal behind their young adult programming is to connect young people to each other with the ultimate goal of pulling them into the larger mission of the church. She explained that Old St. Pat's views the young adult ministry as successful when young adults become part of the other programs in the church, such as involvement in the liturgy, leading ministries or even serving on the finance committee. In fact, their staff includes a number of young adult members in their twenties and thirties.

Krista Kutz, one of the liturgy ministers, who is in her late-twenties, comments that they often hear when people walk into a baptism preparation course that they expect an elderly volunteer who will pass out handouts but at Old St. Pat's they encounter an young woman in her late twenties who is energetic and excited about liturgy. Krista believes that having young ministers interested in liturgy allows other young adults to relate, especially when the ministers look like them and sometimes have friends that work in similar jobs to theirs. She thinks that this helps to break down stereotypes and provides a new, inviting face to the Catholic Church.

Old St. Pat's approaches young adults as their own subpopulation of the community, while also recognizing that they are part of the collective community and should not be isolated. Towards this end, they use a broad definition of "young adults" that does not limit it to single and unmarried people in their twenties and thirties. As Fr. Hurley notes, too often "young adults ministry" is a singles ministry program but in reflecting on the young adults in his parish he notes they are also married couples and young parents. Therefore, while they do develop programming aimed at a more narrow population that includes going to bars to discuss theology, they also recognize that much of their programming involves opportunities to minister to young adults more broadly.

Integrating young adult programming and ministry into the overall philosophy of the church and not isolating them within the community has tied the success of the young adult ministry to the success of the congregation. One young adult who regularly attends commented that he believes the vibrancy of the young adult population is a result of the vibrancy of the overall congregation. In describing his involvement, he included examples of attending both events aimed at young adults, such as walking to a local bar after the 5:00 pm service to discuss spiritual matters, and events that crossed generations, such as serving on a social justice committee. As a result, Old St. Pat's was able to holistically serve his spiritual needs.

What We Can Learn from Old St. Patrick's Church

In many ways Old St. Pat's is a unique congregation that could appear difficult to replicate. The convenient location that allows people to easily commute to it, the historically beautiful building that draws couples seeking to get married there, or its history as a revered institution of the city, are all facets that cannot be easily reproduced. It is important to remember, however, that Old St. Pat's was once a struggling congregation with only four members and that their careful attention to young adults helped them to grow. The history and current ministry of Old St. Pat's offers insight into various principles of successful programming with young adults in their twenties and thirties.

First, Old St. Pat's actively embraces their faith tradition. Both young adults and staff commented on the fact that the staff really enjoy liturgy. Their passion for the music, liturgy and rituals of the church results in religious education programs that do not involve blandly recounting the rules of the church, but instead offer peers that enthusiastically and intelligently discuss the traditions in ways that highlight the continued relevance. Rather than approach the Catholic Church's traditions as something to avoid or downplay with young adults, they find a way to make them a strength and something to take pride in. The staff explained that they adopt an attitude of being open to questions and believe that the ensuing discussions can make Catholicism more understandable.

A second related point is that Old St. Pat's takes pride in offering compelling and high-quality services. Across the city, the church is known for having services that involve relevant preaching and beautiful music. One young adult, after attending a service at Old St. Pat's for the first time, commented that he recognized all the hymns from the Catholic Church he grew up in but that he had never heard them performed so beautifully. Rather than change the music and make it sound more like music he would listen to on the radio, he appreciated how the Old St. Pat's choir had infused traditional hymns with new life. He commented that for young Catholics, the music performed at Old St. Pat's is simultaneously familiar and fresh. As a result, attending Old St. Pat's connects young Catholics to their own faith histories but also makes attending Mass feel new and compelling, creating a more moving experience.

A third insight from Old St. Pat's is the fact that to attract young adults, a church does not have to try to "sell themselves" and compete with other marketing aimed at young adults. As Keara Ette explained, young adults are in high demand and constantly encounter people trying to sell things to them. Rather than try to make church "hip" by changing the music and creating a separate young adult-style service, Old St. Pat's has chosen to provide everyone a high-quality service and a welcoming community. This approach sends the message that the church wants to integrate young adults as people rather than as a demographic. In practice this has meant that they do not have a curriculum-based approach to young adult ministry but instead a relationship-based approach. Rather than design their programming around either the church's narrow boxes or a narrow image of young adults, they emphasize creating programs that emerge from discussions with real young adults. By focusing on producing a quality service and not a cheesy facsimile of church, young adults are approached as the next generation that church must seriously invest in.

A fourth related point that the Old St. Pat's approach indicates is that sometimes churches must reframe their attitudes towards young adults. Rather than view the transitory lives of young adults as a sign of lack of commitment or faith, Ette notes that this is a product of their life position. Young adults' lives are often externally structured by jobs and school in ways that mean their schedules and living situations can be unpredictable and ever-changing. Instead of feeling resentful that young adults may not be able to be clear in how long they can commit their time and energy, she encourages churches to redesign some of their commitments to accommodate the unique life situations of young adults.

Old St. Pat's realized that in order to create the space for young adults to be able to serve on committees they had to reevaluate the type of commitments they expected. Specifically, they recognized that typical three-year commitments were prohibitive to the involvement of many young adults. Ette explains that sometimes a young adult can be an amazing contributing member for only eight months and they leave because they have to move for school. Rather than view this as a limitation to working with young adults, she encourages other churches to value these contributions and accept this as part of the process of ministering to young adults. In particular, Ette encourages churches to view young adult ministries as a long-term process and commitment on the part of the church. Learning about young adults and involving them with the life of the church involves building real relationships with young adults, and that that requires time, as well as recognizing that they have complicated lives with many demands. Creating a successful young adult ministry does not mean finding one group of committed young adults, but rather creating a church that is always inviting new people to participate.

By viewing young adults as a group of people to build long-term relationships with, instead of a demographic to be marketed to, a fifth insight Old St. Pat's offers is a way to approach integrating young adults into the church community. Rather than focus on creating a vibrant but parallel ministry for young adults that includes their own isolated programs and services, the Old St. Pat's philosophy is to use young adult programming as a way to serve the needs of this population with the goal of bringing them into the overall church community. While the church frequently reflects on their level of service to the young adult population, Fr. Hurley strongly believes that this should be contextualized within thinking about the needs of the whole community.

One way they do this is by using a broad definition of young adults that does not serve only unmarried individuals but rather recognizes that the "young adult" demographic is broad with varying needs and desires that can include everything from drinking at bars to childcare for young parents. They also recognize the points where young adult needs overlap with the general community, such as creating compelling services that are responsive to current issues. Another way they integrate young adults is by providing spaces both within and outside of young adult ministries for leadership. One young man I spoke with commented that he went to a lecture at the church about social justice which he found particularly moving and that afterwards he contacted the church about how he could be part of their effort on this topic. Now, he is on a multi-generational committee devoted to social justice. Old St. Pat's intentionally considers the young adult perspective and seeks to build relationships with people in this demographic, but they also realize that their needs are tied to the community at large.

Finally, the Old St. Pat's practice of inreach programming serves as a reminder that young adults are reaching out to the church and these represent ripe opportunities for the church to build relationships. As part of the larger ethos of hospitality at the church, Old St. Pat's strives to make these times positive and welcoming. By using their own married couples during marriage preparation classes, they provide young adults with a friendly face and set of stories about what belonging to the church can be like. Additionally, they adopt a position that is open to questions and does not view them as a sign of disrespect or as a challenge but as an opportunity to make the beliefs, rules, and rituals of the Catholic Church meaningful to a new generation.

In talking to young adults (staff, locals and members), two things struck me. First, the church found ways to structure programming around activities that young adults were already interested in. Numerous times staff commented that events like the Block Party or Theology on Tap were the type of activities that young adults already do and Old St. Pat's was trying to find a way to make church relevant in their lives by hosting similar events. Second, the church sought to capitalize on the times when young adults might come in contact with the church, specifically weddings. Again, as the staff noted frequently, young adults are getting married and having kids. They viewed these as life events that the church could make itself more relevant to, and not just an item to check-off the list.

These six insights – embracing one's faith tradition; quality services; avoiding marketing to young adults; building authentic relationships; integrating young adults into the community, and capitalizing on moments when young adults reach out to the church – have been important for the success of not only the young adult ministry at Old St. Pat's but the church overall. Even while other elements of the congregation may be difficult to replicate, these six elements provide useful directions for other churches to pursue in their attempt to reach out to younger generations.

Courtney Ann Irby is a doctoral candidate in the department of sociology at Loyola University Chicago. Her work focuses on understanding the religious lives of young adults, including studying how young evangelicals draw on their faith communities to understand and form romantic relationships.

References

Skerret, Ellen, ed. 1997. *At the Crossroads: Old Saint Patrick's and the Chicago Irish*. Chicago, IL: Wild Onion Books. (A book commemorating the 150th anniversary of Old St. Pat's Church, it includes a number of essays about the history of the parish.)

Wedam, Elfriede. 2000. "Catholic Spirituality in a New Urban Church." Pp. 212-238 in *Public Religion and Urban Transformation: Faith in the City*, ed. Lowell W. Livezey. New York: New York University Press. (A sociological study of Old St. Pat's that analyzes its history that considers how the church responded to and created a new type of urban parish.)

Old St. Patrick's web site: http://oldstpats.org/

Facebook page for Old St. Patrick's:
https://www.facebook.com/OldStPatricksChurch?fref=ts

Lonely Planet web site:
www.lonelyplanet.com/usa/chicago/sights/other/old-st-patrick#ixzz2Y2DoTBvY

Chapter 10
Saint Mary Orthodox Church
Cambridge, Massachusetts

By Danielle Xanthos

Saint Mary Antiochian Orthodox Church in Cambridge, Massachusetts is a diverse, vibrant, and unique community led by Father Antony Hughes. An exploration of the young adult population was conducted through the interview of both young and seasoned generations, as well as leaders and general parishioners. As this community is highly active in academia, and observations for this report were made during the demanding time of finals, holidays, and the start to a new semester, a variation of reports may be found at another time.

St. Mary's is a particularly interesting case study regarding young adults. While there is a high percentage of people 18 to 29 years old (well over 25 percent on a typical Sunday Divine Liturgy), there are no specific ministries targeted for this age group. Instead, ministries tend to be open to all, such as the national ministry of the Fellowship of Saint John the Divine. This Orthodox parish was selected based on the consistent attendance of young people, their knowledge of their faith, and the integral role they play in the St. Mary's community. It is common in ethnic Orthodox parishes to find a significant gap in liturgical attendance between the ages 18-29. St. Mary's is an example by which other Orthodox churches may evaluate the use of language, time of worship, and intent of ministry in their parishes.

Unity in Diversity

In order to better understand diversity in the context of this community, it is necessary to note unique aspects of Orthodox Christianity. In tandem with unity, the Orthodox Faith encompasses a great variety of regional customs and traditions. Centers of Early Christianity emerged from the very beginning of Apostolic times through the fifth century. These centers, known as the "pentarchy" or five sees, are regions of significant events and influential teachers, including Rome, Constantinople, Alexandria, Antioch and Jerusalem. As the Christian world expanded, regions of Eastern Europe, Asia, and Africa received the faith. As a result of the high influx of Eastern European and Middle Eastern immigration to the United States in the 19th century, Orthodox communities in America tend to maintain, to various degrees, their ethnic background. For this reason, Greek, Arab, Russian, Serbian, Albanian, Ukrainian, Romanian, and Bulgarian Orthodox churches exist in America, yet it is important to note the unity among these nationalities as the one Orthodox Church. In addition, a reported 23 percent of Orthodox Christians in America are converts. (Pew: US Religious Landscape) Considering the diversity within Orthodoxy, this report on the young adult population of St. Mary Antiochian Orthodox Church cannot be considered a typical portrait of Orthodox parishes, but a lively tile in the mosaic of Orthodoxy.

History of the Community

The community of St. Mary's was founded in 1928 by Syrian immigrants who eventually purchased a Boston school building and converted it into a church. Until the arrival of Fr. John von Holzhausen in 1945, services were predominantly in Arabic. The task of Fr. John was to introduce English into the liturgical life of the church. By 17 years after St. Mary's founding, the common language had become English. The switch to English was quite revolutionary in the ethnic Orthodox parish of the 1940's and resulted in an increased attendance in young people. The community accepted the reality that the young people were no longer immigrants, but mostly first generation English-speaking Americans. Due to continual growth, the community purchased and consecrated the current Cambridge church building in 1954. The tall-steepled white church is still ornamented with brilliant pre-Civil War stained glass and solid oak pews.

Cambridge is home to about 105,000 people (U.S. Census), and along with its neighboring city of Boston, home to over 250,000 students. St. Mary's is located in the very heart of Cambridge, approximately a mile from the Massachusetts Institute of Technology (MIT) and Harvard University. Students can easily access St. Mary's with the Massachusetts Bay Transportation Authority (MBTA) by subway or bus. From MIT, travel is an 8-minute bus ride down Massachusetts Avenue. Harvard University students may travel on the Red Line from Central Square Station to Harvard Square, reaching the doors of St. Mary's in just seven minutes. Easy accessibility for college and graduate students is a major advantage contributing to the vibrant young adult population of St. Mary's.

While Cambridge is heavily populated with students, there is also a great prevalence of homelessness. It is difficult to walk a block without being asked for change. It is not unusual for a homeless person to come through the doors or St. May's during coffee hour. Some members of the community engage in conversation while others remain distant, illustrating an ambivalent attitude toward homelessness in Cambridge. One young adult notes walking along Massachusetts Avenue after a service during which red roses were distributed by the clergy. A short distance from the church, a homeless person was holding a rose given to him by a parishioner.

Services and Statistics

The evening prayer service of Great Vespers is held every Saturday at 5pm, with the option to have the sacrament of confession at 6 pm or by appointment. Each Sunday from September through June the morning prayer service of Orthros begins at 8:45am, followed by Divine Liturgy at 10am. During the months of July and August, Orthros begins at 8:15 am, followed by Divine Liturgy at 9:45 am. On the eve of feast days of the Church, vesperal liturgies are held at 6:30 pm. This is a pragmatic solution to schedule conflicts of weekday morning services, provided by the blessing of the Antiochian

Archdiocese. Typically, an estimated 20 people are in attendance at vesperal liturgies.

On Holy Saturday [the day before Easter Sunday] morning the church is filled with young people. At this time, catechumens are baptized at St. Mary's. In the past there have been as many as 25 people received into the Orthodox Church on Holy Saturday. The church seats 500 on the floor level and 250 on the balcony. There are currently 137 pledging families, though many others who are not "members" attend services. On a typical Sunday, an average of 250 attend Liturgy. On a particular Sunday prior to the spring academic semester, of the 154 people in attendance, 38, or 25 percent, were young adults. As recorded by leadership observation, growth in the past five years has flourished. Thirteen people are currently enrolled in the catechism class. Fr. Antony reports, "The people coming in are young, and many of them are not Orthodox."

While twenty-three nationalities have been represented among the faithful, English is recognized as the common language of the community. In a multi-ethnic and pan-Orthodox parish, the use of English allows young people to understand and learn the faith through liturgical life. While the majority of prayers and hymns are in English, there is use of Arabic, Greek, and, to a lesser extent, other languages.

Growth of Young Adult Attendance

A parishioner since 1980, Charlie M., shares his experience of moving from New Jersey to Boston as an undergraduate at MIT. He admits being advised not attend St. Mary's on account of a weak young adult ministry. He attended St. George Antiochian Orthodox Church of Boston, located in West Roxbury. While he attended with friends, this was a tedious commute. Citing a change in public transportation services, Charlie began riding his bike to St. Mary's just as the newly assigned Fr. Gregory Phalen set a welcoming environment. Charlie recalls only three college students attending at the time, though as Fr. Gregory's mission to preach the gospel gained momentum, there was a greater desire and capacity to learn what it means to be Orthodox. A catechumen class was developed and the tone of the parish became one of sharing the Orthodox faith, not only with newcomers, but also with those who had been baptized during infancy.

This rebuilding of the community marked the start of the young adult ministry. Charlie reflects on the great impact Fr. Gregory had on him, the community, and the other young people. As a convert, Fr. Gregory preached the gospel in a way that had a different character. He focused on attracting young people, recognizing the need to show an interest in them. For young people raised in religious community, college often marks a time in life in which church attendance is no longer an obligation but a conscious decision. Charlie recalls thinking as a college student, "If you come to church and hear a good message, you'll keep coming back." Fr. Gregory seemed to recognize this, and valuing the Sunday morning of college students, he put great effort into his ministry. Fr. Gregory's ministry is marked by a reestablishment of liturgical life, a high percentage of young adults attending Saturday vespers, the celebration of vesperal liturgies, allowing people to attend services without conflicts of their work day, and an increase in celebrating feast days. The changes brought lasting effects of growth in understanding services and traditions.

Fr. Gregory provided the Harvard University chapter of the Orthodox Christian Fellowship (OCF) with a chaplain. The OCF is a nationwide collegiate campus ministry organization under the Assembly of Canonical Orthodox Bishops of North and South America. OCF provides Orthodox Christian college students with the opportunity to grow in faith and friendship through prayer, service, and fellowship. From the time of Fr. Gregory's death in 1989, Fr. Alexis Khoury continued the campus ministry of OCF, as well as starting a new chapter at MIT with Charlie and his wife. By 1990, there were six OCF chapters in Boston, at Tufts University, Northeastern

University, Boston University, Boston College, Harvard and MIT.

In 1993, Fr. Antony Hughes was assigned to St. Mary's. Fr. Antony was chaplain of the OCF chapters at both MIT and Harvard. With a great number of colleges and universities, as well as Orthodox parishes of various jurisdictions, many young people have been exposed to the pan-Orthodox spirit of the area. OCF gives students the opportunity to experience both the diversity and unity of the Orthodox faith. After six years of this service, Fr. Antony resigned from his duties as OCF chaplain, explaining, "When students started coming to church, I realized this is where I can really do the ministry to the college students." At this point in the 1990's, approximately 20 college students were attending services at St. Mary's regularly.

Ministering to the Cambridge community, a highly educated and motivated setting, it is beneficial for the leaders of the parish to have knowledge of academia. Fr. Antony is passionate about learning. With a degree in sociology, he highly appreciates and incorporates the fields of psychology and neuroscience into his ministry. Drawing on modern psychology and meditation, he lights up when speaking about dialectical behavior therapy, unconditional positive regard, and mindfulness practices. An empirical understanding of young adults informs the unique way in which he ministers to them. He recognizes the unique needs of the young people who come into the community, "Different people are at different places in their lives," he observes.

Mindfulness practices emphasize the experience of the present moment to be crucial in our overall human experience. Fr. Antony applies this in ministry in order to "meet the need that presents itself." By incorporating concepts such as mindfulness into his sermons and connecting them with the teachings of examples, such as St. Isaac the Syrian and St. Gregory Palamas, he invites young people to understand the Gospel of Jesus Christ as relevant to the world in which we live. In doing so, he encourages awareness of the presence of God in every single moment of their lives. Contrary to what many young people assume, Fr. Antony believes, "There is nothing more relevant than the Gospel of Jesus Christ," but it must be preached and lived. He shares, "I teach a very practical spirituality, and that's what young people crave." The community of St. Mary's does not fear the secular world. Instead, they embrace it through the filter of their Orthodox faith.

Finances

The late 1990's marked a low point in parish finances. At this time, dues were no longer required and a new stewardship program was enacted. This program was based on the individual or family's ability. As a result, St. Mary's experienced a great increase in pledges, which significantly helped the financial stability of the community. This change was based on scriptural teachings of offering according to ability. To date, the community does not spend a great amount, as it relies mostly on volunteer work. In fact, the budget information contains no expenses for young adult ministry. Income circulates through stewardship donations and hall rentals, which help to offset costs. According to the 2012 annual budget report, the actual income was $53, 889.

Change

As more young people began to regularly attend services in the 1990's, the older Syrian generation questioned the seriousness of young adults regarding their faith and community. Transition occurred with the forming of the Fellowship of St. John the Divine. Young adults took a great stride in immersing themselves in the community when dozens of young people attended a parish council meeting asking, "We're here to serve you. What is it that we can do?" The young generation took on the work the older generation had been doing each Sunday for 50 years. It simply began when the older generation asked the young group to put the chairs away after coffee hour. This offering of service allowed the older people to recognize the readiness of the young people to contribute to their Church. The older ethnic generation embraces and educates the young people through their faithful practice of the Orthodox Tradition.

Program Philosophy

The spirit of tradition lives through a personal relationship between generations. Transition of leadership is passed down in a unique way through education concerning both the history and ethnicity of the parish. Through the liturgical life, coffee hour, community meals, and various other events, young people offer their service to the older generation. There are no ministries specific to young adults at St. Mary's. This is reflective of the community's unique interconnectedness between and among generations. Young adults are involved in various capacities of church life, in contrast to the common assumption that age dictates one's role in the community. Age-specific programs do not fit the life of St. Mary's. Fr. Antony reasons, "It is the organic life of the community... the program is at work all the time; It's the love of the community."

Programs are not limited to particular age groups, but are open to all. The Fellowship of Saint John the Divine, a program of the Antiochian Orthodox Christian Archdiocese, is focused on the unity, missions, outreach, evangelism and spiritual renewal of members. Through the Fellowship, the community comes together to participate in the liturgical life in numerous ways: by reading the Epistle, holding the Communion cloth and blessed bread, greeting parishioners and visitors as they enter the church, sponsoring coffee hour, cleaning the hall, organizing meals for College Students' Welcome Back, Meatfare Sunday, Palm Sunday, and Easter, organizing the Father John vonHolzhausen lecture series, organizing potluck dinners following Pre-Sanctified Liturgies throughout Lent, and decorating the hall and Church for Feast Days. (Church Web site, "Fellowship")

The surrounding community of Cambridge is active in social outreach. This is an interest that is infused within the individuals of the church. Considering the Syrian ethnic background of the parish, the community of St. Mary's honors a great sensitivity to political outreach. Young community members are socially conscious and provide outreach to a local battered women's shelter, Open Door Ministry (a ministry of Holy Resurrection Bulgarian Orthodox Church in Allston, MA through which dinners are served, with dignity, to the hungry), training to serve the Orthodox Christian Prison Ministry with Deacon Jeff, and through the International Orthodox Christian Charities and the Orthodox Christian Mission Center. Through these outreach ministries, there is an awareness of what Fr. Antony describes as, "traditions and transitions."

Influence of Orthodox Youth, Camp, and College Ministries

The active young people at St. Mary's are highly influenced by youth and college ministries. Many young people come to St. Mary's because of their experience of the Orthodox network of camp ministry. During the 1990's and 2000's, Fr. Antony was highly active with Antiochian Village, camp ministry of Antiochian Orthodox Christian Archdiocese of North America located in Bolivar, Pennsylvania. His role as clergy at the camp made a significant impact on many campers who have now grown to young adulthood. Through Antiochian Village, many young people are familiar with Fr. Antony and the community of St. Mary's. This has been instrumental in attracting young adults to the parish. In recent years, Fr. Antony has served the Greek Orthodox Metropolis of Boston Summer Camp in Contoocook, New Hampshire.

Young Orthodox people are exposed to St. Mary's through other programs such as CrossRoad, a summer institute for high school juniors and seniors located on the campus of Hellenic College Holy Cross Greek Orthodox School of Theology in Brookline, Massachusetts. During the CrossRoad program, participants are exposed to the diversity of Orthodoxy by visiting parishes of all Orthodox jurisdictions throughout the Boston area. During the past summer's visit to St. Mary's, participants celebrated vespers, followed by Fr. Antony's sharing of his own journey, as a Southern Baptist, toward Orthodoxy.

Exposure to St. Mary's also occurs through participation of parishioners and clergy at various OCF programs such as College Conference and Real Break. College Conference brings hundreds of Orthodox students together at Antiochian Village and Saint Nicholas Ranch in California annually. In the past, Fr. Antony has presented workshops at College Conference. His workshop on meditation drew over a hundred students. He plans to continue to attend the Conference in coming years. Real Break provides college students the opportunity to experience the world through service and learning in Greece, Alaska, Romania, Guatemala, Jerusalem, Constantinople, El Salvador, Puerto Rico, and Mexico, among others. At the time of this writing, St. Mary's is working to build a church and tend to an orphanage in El Salvador.

Clergy from around the country encourage their young people to attend services at St. Mary's. Involvement of clergy and parishioners in ministries of the Orthodox world has allowed St. Mary's to become a well-known parish throughout the country. However, because of the large percentage of students, the young adult population has a transient nature. Each year, college and graduate students complete their programs, often leaving the Boston area, and new students are welcomed.

Transience of Young People

Adam M., a college freshman, expresses this phenomenon of transience as an attribute that encourages the "different flavor" of St. Mary's. There is a constant rotation of young people each year and due to this, St. Mary's provides "a different feel at any given time by the different people who are there." He describes this as potentially good or bad. There is a danger of new members taking on too much responsibility without learning the dynamics of the community, yet it also provides the community with new ideas. Adam, whose family converted to Orthodoxy when he was two years old, grew up attending St. Mary's until moving at the age of twelve. He returned to Boston to attend college and chose to make St. Mary's his home parish once again. St. Mary provides a great opportunity for learning Byzantine chant and for his study of liturgics. Adam chants during Orthros and, as a subdeacon, serves in the Divine Liturgy each Sunday.

Growth and Salvation as an Ongoing Process

Fr. Antony strives to provide a place for young people where "it's safe to be who they are." There is a pastoral, as opposed to legalistic, approach in the ministry of the parish. The uniqueness of each person is honored and the spiritual growth of each person is cultivated. In depicting this, Fr. Antony paraphrases St. Gregory of Nyssa, "The only sin is failure to grow." (Danielou, p. 60) St. Gregory tells of St. Paul's continual growth toward God, "Paul does not let the graces he has obtained become the limit of his desire, but he continues to go on and on, never ceasing his ascent." The environment of St. Mary embraces this constant process of growth of which the fourth century saint speaks.

This sentiment is recognized by the young people of the parish. Steven P., a recent graduate of Harvard graduate studies in philosophy, characterizes the community by its "striving toward complete love for everyone and everything." He goes on to explain how an attitude of openness towards the truth is fostered at St. Mary's, but this truth is not a "stabilized system" by which one declares, "Finally, I've arrived."

Steven explains, "Truth is always challenging you in an uncomfortable way." While attending St. Mary's, he has come to understand, "Christianity is love and openness, but not in a way that is easy… it's a lot more difficult than following a set of rules." In his own spiritual journey, Steven recognizes his imperfection. Through Fr. Antony's sermons and his own academic pursuits in philosophy and theology, Steven has reflected a greater understanding of Orthodoxy since his conversion as a college freshman in 2005.

Oftentimes, he observes a zealous enthusiasm in the newly Orthodox that wanes when "things get tough." He notes that a possible cause of this may be due to idealization and idolization of a faith rather than genuine desire for transformation. At St. Mary's, Steven says, the faithful are challenged to "approach the Word with a sense of awe and wonder, even in the most insignificant…and dark moments of life." He appreciates the challenge to "open your eyes to see the beauty of the world."

Fellowship

St. Mary's provides a community of fellowship that extends beyond official Church events. Whether watching a Patriots game together or sharing an apartment, young adults find friendships in the warm environment. Tom P., a 27-year-old high school teacher, describes the young people of St. Mary's as "down-to-earth; they like to have fun but are also very serious about their religion." Tom was raised Episcopalian until the age of 7, when his family converted. While living in Boston during the 1970's, decades prior to his conversion to Orthodoxy, Tom's father had visited St. Mary's during Holy Week. Tom attributes his choice to continue attending St. Mary's to the liturgical practices of the kiss of peace, the warmth of Fr. Antony, and the network of people, both young and old. As a member of the Fellowship of St. John the Divine, Tom shares in the various events organized by the group. These events cultivate a sense of fellowship through coffeehouse events, talent shows, and decorating the Church. He is also involved in teaching the Sunday Church School.

There are various key elements of the community that people like Tom find appealing. Among those is the approachability of Fr. Antony. Each morning Fr. Antony sends a daily text message of inspiration and thought from various fields such as theology, psychology, or literature. Another key element is the diversity that reaches many levels. The great variety of professionals allows young people to develop relationships with mentors who have similar interests and careers. The diversity of people includes those from Syrian, Romanian, Ethiopian, Russian, Greek, Lebanese, Palestinian, Italian, and Eritrean people. Taking the opportunity to sit at one of the many vibrant tables during coffee hour exposes young people to unique stories of different lives, from which much can be gained. Through these relationships the diversity of the world is witnessed in the unity of Orthodoxy.

As a graduate student of Social Work at Boston College, Jerred E. reflects on his journey through Orthodoxy. Jerred was baptized into Orthodoxy in Wichita, Kansas, during his infancy; however, his family soon moved a two-hour distance from an Orthodox Church. While growing up in Indiana, he explored different churches with his Protestant friends. In his adolescence, Jerred began to learn about Orthodoxy through the camp ministry of Antiochian Village, where he met Fr. Antony. Antiochian Village provided Jerred with an Orthodox setting that he could not experience within a two-hour drive from home. He continued to grow in his faith through Antiochian Village until attending college at Purdue University, where he was involved in OCF. During college, Jerred kept in contact with Fr. Antony through weekly phone calls and care packages.

As a child, Jerred considered the ordained priesthood. Fr. Antony was open to dialogue about the priesthood while honoring Jerred's freedom to decide his own path. He came to realize his priestly vocation was outside of the ordained priesthood. Learning about eastern practices of martial arts and meditation, Jerred shares the words of French Eastern Orthodox theologian Olivier Clement, "Not a blade of grass grows outside the Church." Jerred's interests lie in mindfulness-based therapy, stating, "To be mindful is to be present... God is in the moment." He relates his study of mindfulness to the practice of Orthodoxy, recognizing "the Kingdom of Heaven is at hand." Emphasizing the impacts this understanding has on the way in which one chooses to live right now, he explains that the Kingdom of Heaven is happening here and now, as a process.

Dena F. was baptized Catholic and grew up in a Protestant mega-church in California. She was introduced to Orthodoxy by a friend in high school, and is continuing her journey toward the Orthodox Church as a catechumen. After college she lived in Bulgaria for a year, where she began attending the Divine Liturgy every Sunday. She is currently living in Cambridge as a Ph. D. student of English at Harvard University. Upon moving to the Boston area, Orthodox friends suggested she attend St. Mary's, where she quickly felt welcomed,

"I definitely felt way more at home and part of the community when I walked in," she says. "I could have gone to another Orthodox church in the area, but I wouldn't find this sort of network of people who are studying what I am studying." Dena feels comfortable and at home, instead of feeling like an outsider.

Having only been to Greek and Bulgarian churches, she has an appreciation for the slightly different style of the Antiochian parish. As a young person attending St. Mary's with the intention of converting to Orthodoxy, Dena appreciates the mix of old and new generations. The older generation provides wisdom and experience to guide young people toward a healthy and balanced faith.

The first sermon Dena heard at St. Mary's was Fr. Antony speaking against fundamentalism. As a convert himself, Fr. Antony is aware of the "traps that people can fall into" during their conversion into the Church. In that same sermon, he spoke against superstition, which often has a stronghold in more ethnic populations. She feels, "I can be myself in this environment."

As a Ph.D. student, Dena is encouraged by Fr. Antonly's words, "Our theology is expansive and dynamic and not afraid of knowledge. As long as our message to the world is reactionary, then we will be afraid of knowledge." Encouraging young people to challenge the common belief that faith and our modern world are in opposition, she recalls the sermon as saying, "Orthodoxy offers so much to postmodern culture." Emphasizing metanoia, she quotes Fr. Antony, "Repentance is to change one's mind; Fundamentalism is incompatible with metanoia."

Entering into the St. Mary's community from a Greek Orthodox background was challenge, at first, for Jenelle M., a young Boston optometrist. Initially focused on the high use of English and more western-style iconography, she felt distant from the service. However, over time, the acceptance and welcome into the community allowed her to experience the parish in a different way. With the service in English, even for a modern Greek-speaker, she was better able to connect spiritually as she understood the service on a different level. She notes the consistency of attendance. A relatively high percentage of young people attend Orthros prior to the Divine Liturgy. Young adults accounted for 30 percent of attendance for the morning service. Throughout the year, a comparable number of people are present during Holy Week service as compared to attendance on a typical Sunday. In many ethnic churches, this is not the case. The colloquial term "Chreaster," used to describe those who attend church only on Christmas and Easter, simply does not apply to St. Mary's. There is a great consistency that displays a genuine worship in the life of St. Mary's.

While St. Mary's provides an example of successful ministry, it is important to recognize the uniqueness of the Cambridge area. The transience of the young people allow those of ethnic Orthodox backgrounds to freely practice their faith in a pan-

Orthodox way. Each interview credited Fr. Antony as a great influence in the consistent attendance of young adults. He leads his community by example of love and awareness of the Gospel through the warmth he provides to all. This community exhibits the importance of faith, fellowship, unity, and diversity.

This case study of St. Mary's provides an example of an Orthodox parish in which a population is booming. Further studies of young people in other Orthodox communities would allow for a greater understanding of why young people choose to remain, leave, or enter the Church. Considering the great student population, one might question where the other Orthodox students may be. Further studies as to why Orthodox students choose not to attend church services regularly would provide insight for the Church's outreach to young people.

Danielle Xanthos is currently working toward her Master of Divinity degree and holds a Bachelor of Science in Psychology. She has extensive experience in youth ministry and intends on entering the clinical mental health field.

References

Antiochian Orthodox Christian Archdiocese of North America,
http://www.antiochian.org/

Antiochian Village,
http://www.antiochianvillage.org/center.html

Danielou, J. (1961) *From Glory to Glory: Texts from Gregory of Nyssa's Mystical Writings.* New York: Charles Scribner's Sons.

CrossRoad,
http://www.hchc.edu/studentlife/vocation/crossroad

Orthodox Christian Fellowship, http://www.ocf.net/

Sermons,
http://www.stmaryorthodoxchurch.org/orthodoxy/sermons.php

St. Mary Antiochian Orthodox Church,
http://www.stmaryorthodoxchurch.org/index.php

U.S. Census Bureau (2013). State and County QuickFacts. Retrieved from
http://quickfacts.census.gov/qfd/states/25/2511000.html

Chapter 11
Next *Dor* DC at Temple Micah
Washington DC

By Ramie Arian

This case study profiles a project called Next *Dor* DC, a program to engage people in their 20s and 30s sponsored by Temple Micah (hereinafter sometimes referred to simply as "Micah"), a Reform Jewish congregation located at 2829 Wisconsin Avenue NW, Washington DC 20007. The clergy team of Temple Micah is headed by Rabbi Daniel G. Zemel, senior rabbi. Rabbi Esther L. Lederman is assistant rabbi, and holds principle responsibility for guiding Next *Dor* DC. (*Dor* is a Hebrew word meaning "generation.")

In 2009, the congregation was named by *Newsweek* as one of the 25 most dynamic Jewish congregations in the United States. The congregation's website offers this description: "Temple Micah… is a Reform Jewish congregation dedicated to the spiritual fulfillment of its members. We value religious observance enhanced by social action, intellectual challenge, lifelong Jewish learning and beautiful music. Our diverse and welcoming community nurtures personal connections through active participation in a vibrant temple life." (Temple Micah web site)

Elsewhere on the website, the description continues: "Temple Micah is a teaching, caring and doing congregation. We are at once traditional and innovative, combining a good helping of time-honored ritual with groundbreaking, new approaches to Jewish life. We put a premium on creativity, experimentation and learning. We urge every member to join us in a meaningful religious journey and to build personal connections through active participation in the life of our community… We have fun. We delight in delicious food, and raise money by preparing gourmet meals for each other. Exquisite music adds beauty and emotional richness to our services…"

Key Data

Temple Micah currently has some 520 member families. Regular worship is held every Shabbat (Sabbath), with services on Friday evening and Saturday morning, and on Jewish holidays. Typically, Temple Micah hosts approximately 100 worshipers on Friday evening. On Saturday mornings when there is no Bar/Bat Mitzvah, attendance is in the range of 40-50; when there is a Bar/Bat Mitzvah, attendance ranges from 125-250, depending on the number of guests. As is typical in Jewish congregations, worship attendance for the High Holidays (Rosh Hashana and Yom Kippur, which occur in the Fall, 10 days apart) is significantly higher, usually by a factor of at least 10. (Bar Mitzvah [for boys] and Bat Mitzvah [for girls] are coming-of-age ceremonies which are celebrated around the 13th birthday. It is typical for the family of the young person being so honored to invite a large number of guests to attend the Shabbat morning service, and to host a reception which follows.)

Temple Micah conducts regular Shabbat evening worship on Friday evenings at 6:30, preceded by an Oneg Shabbat at 6. Literally translated as "joy of the Sabbath," an Oneg Shabbat is a light collation which presents an opportunity for socializing in connection with worship. Micah's choice to offer the Oneg Shabbat prior to worship is unusual; most Jewish congregations hold an Oneg Shabbat following worship. Shabbat morning worship is at 10:15 on Saturdays.

Temple Micah designates the second Shabbat of each month as Next *Dor* Sabbath. On those occasions, next-generation participants represent 15% to 20% of the congregation. Special programs conducted for the Next *Dor* DC group generally attract 20 to 30 participants.

Over the past five years, the Temple's membership has been growing by about 25 families, or about 5%, per year. The congregation has some 40 members who are in their 20s and 30s whose membership can be attributed directly to their participation in Next *Dor* DC, though Temple Micah is explicit that increasing membership is **not** a goal of the Next *Dor* DC program (see below). Another 15 people in this age cohort have joined as members of the congregation, but subsequently relocated away from the DC area. This represents a 10-fold increase in membership in this age cohort from before the advent of the Next *Dor* DC program.

As the Temple Micah constituency is overwhelmingly English-speaking, all activities are conducted in English. As is typical in Jewish congregations, worship is conducted in a combination of English and Hebrew.

Demographics and Culture

Temple Micah has never had deep connections with its neighborhood, but rather has always been something of a "destination synagogue" which serves Jews from all around the District of Columbia and its environs who are looking for an unconventional and forward-thinking approach to Jewish life. At one time, the synagogue printed bumper stickers which read: "Temple Micah: It's Worth the Schlep." ("Schlep" is a Yiddish word which roughly translates as "trek.")

The constituency of the congregation is largely Caucasian, though there is a notable minority of Jews of color. In general, the community is a well-educated constituency of professional class, college graduates. The community includes many interfaith families, and many Jews-by-choice. The District of Columbia is a gathering place for people who come from many places of origin, and Temple Micah is no exception. A significant number of participants are essentially transient, arriving (and expecting to depart) with the incumbent political administration. The community is of mixed economic means, from working class to wealthy. The congregation attracts Jews from a mixture of professions, notably including government workers, teachers, lawyers, and professionals in the large DC not-for-profit sector.

Background and History

Temple Micah was established in 1963 by a group of young Jews who had moved to the District of Columbia in the early 1960s, propelled by the visions of Presidents John F. Kennedy's New Frontier and Lyndon B. Johnson's Great Society. Its founders envisioned that Temple Micah would be a Jewish voice for what its members were doing in their professional lives. From the beginning, the congregation strove to be "not your parents' synagogue." Originally located in the Southwest quadrant of DC, Micah partnered with—and met within the building of—St. Augustine's Episcopal Church.

The congregation always described itself as a congregation for "everybody," which was intended to mean that it was not just for "families." This has always been a part of the congregation's history and identity. (In the 1950s and especially in the 1960s, the Jewish community saw a massive demographic shift from the cities to the suburbs, and a corresponding rise in suburban congregations, which catered overwhelmingly to stereotypical nuclear families. Temple Micah set itself apart by intentionally bucking this trend, taking a welcoming stance toward singles and the many others who did not live in "traditional" families.)

The congregation's first two clergy were Rabbi Richard G. Hirsch, founding director of the Religious Action Center of Reform Judaism and honorary life president of the World Union for Progressive Judaism, and Rabbi Bernard Mehlman, now Rabbi Emeritus of Temple Israel of Boston. Rabbis Hirsch and Mehlman are both dynamic, charismatic figures who are noted for their courage and dedication to social action. Rabbi Daniel Zemel has led the congregation since 1983.

Micah moved from its original location at St. Augustine's to its present location near the National Cathedral in 1995. In the 16 years since, the congregation has grown more than four-fold, from 120 to 520 member families.

As the founding membership aged, the congregation began frequently to grapple with the question of how to remain age-diverse. During the summer of 2000, responding to concerns about attracting younger members, Rabbi Zemel and his wife Louise began to invite newcomers and strangers who attended Friday evening services to come back to their home for Shabbat dinner. Usually, the invitees mainly included young people who were in town for one of DC's many summer internships. This developed into a group for young people in their 20s and 30s, which met monthly in the rabbi's home for a program of Jewish text study, discussion and food. The group continued successfully for about one and a half years. Rabbi Zemel endeavored at that time to induce the group to undertake its own leadership. This effort was unsuccessful, and the group foundered and was discontinued. Some years later, when Temple Micah engaged its first, half-time assistant rabbi, she was given responsibility to revive the young adult group, but this effort floundered.

In 2008, Rabbi Zemel was approached by the leadership of a national organization called Synagogue 3000 (S3K), which describes itself as "a catalyst for excellence, empowering congregations and communities to create synagogues that are sacred and vital centers of Jewish life." S3K had identified engagement of the next generation as a key priority for synagogues across North America, and was establishing a pilot program called Next *Dor* to experiment with bringing more people of the 20s and 30s age group into synagogue life. Next *Dor* invited Micah to be one of its first cohort of pilot sites across the United States. As an incentive to participate, S3K offered to pay a portion of the salary for a full-time assistant rabbi, part of whose assignment would be to lead a Next *Dor* group in the congregation.

In response to this opportunity, the congregation made the decision to engage a second, full-time rabbi, and reached out to Esther Lederman, a young rabbi with a strong background in community organizing. She joined Temple Micah as Assistant Rabbi in the summer of 2009. A significant part of her assignment is to provide leadership for Next *Dor* DC, which has been active since her arrival.

The Next *Dor* DC "Ministry"

Rabbis Lederman and Zemel emphasize that Temple Micah's efforts to engage young people in their 20s and 30s is not about offering programs, but rather, about building relationships. Accordingly Micah's initiative begins with one-on-one relationship-building initiated by Rabbi Lederman. She identifies individuals who have visited the synagogue, or who have been referred to her by one of the Next *Dor* group's current participants, or who cross her "radar screen" in any other way. She contacts such persons individually, and invites them to coffee, usually for a 30-minute conversation in a convenient location, usually near their place of work. The discussion focuses on where the individual is from, who they are, what they're interested in, and whether they are looking for something deeper with regard to the Jewish religion or the Jewish community. She makes it clear that she does not have an agenda to "sell" them. Sometimes these conversations are one-off encounters, and she never sees the individual again; sometimes they lead to the individual's decision to connect in some way with the Next *Dor* group, with the synagogue, with the rabbi, or with Jewish life.

As noted above, Temple Micah designates the second Friday evening of each month as Next *Dor* Shabbat, and especially invites young people of the 20s and 30s age group to join the congregation in worship. The synagogue's worship services always have an informal style, and are notable both for the presence of humor and for particular attention to the music, mostly in a style which invites and encourages congregational participation. There is no change to the worship's style or content for Next *Dor* Shabbat, but both of the rabbis report that the presence of a significant cohort in their 20s and 30s generates a distinctly different feeling during the worship experience, as the young people bring their energy, their humor, and their way of being.

Following the worship service on such occasions, the Next *Dor* participants are invited to a casual Shabbat dinner, sometimes going out together to a restaurant, occasionally organized as a pot-luck at a participant's home, but increasingly, staying at the synagogue and ordering in food. These meals are given structure by Rabbi Lederman, as follows: (1) They begin with an icebreaker exercise, usually with a focus on introducing people and learning one another's names. (2) The group shares some songs together. (3) Rabbi Lederman leads a brief study session, usually focusing on the weekly Torah portion (scriptural reading). (4) The meal is shared. (5) There is a focus on connecting people to one another and building relationships.

On occasion, the time and place may shift. Once in a while, this kind of sharing will take place at Havdallah; occasionally it may take place over a Sunday brunch. (Havdallah is a special, brief ceremony held after sundown on Saturday to mark the end of the Sabbath.)

A second kind of gathering for the Next *Dor* DC group is called "Drinks and Drash." ("Drash," pronounced to rhyme with "wash," is a Hebrew word meaning "interpretation," and is used to denote the process of studying and expanding upon a traditional, often Biblical, text.) This is a gathering which generally takes place on the first Monday of each month, and is located at a restaurant/bar which (unlike Temple Micah itself) is easily accessible to the Metro (DC's subway system), and convenient to where many of the participants work. It is publicized to potential participants through an email list which Rabbi Lederman maintains, through Facebook, and the like. The gathering centers on a study session organized, and often (but not always) taught by Rabbi Lederman, on various timely topics. Such topics have included: Religion in the Public Square; Judaism and Food Justice; and Jews in the Military. Discussion of politics is avoided.

About four times a year, the Next *Dor* DC group undertakes to participate in a social action project. These are typically one-off, hands-on projects. Examples are helping to paint a school, volunteering for a local social-service organization, and working at Micah House, a synagogue-owned half-way house for women coming out of homelessness or addiction. Rabbi Lederman notes that social action projects are less important for the Next *Dor* DC group than they might be for a comparable group in another city, as social action is what many of the participants are engaged with professionally.

Temple Micah sponsors special Next *Dor* worship services on the evenings of the High Holidays Rosh Hashanah and Yom Kippur. Attendance at these services is open without membership and without paid tickets. The services are conducted in the main sanctuary of Temple Micah by Rabbi Lederman and a visiting guest musician (the main services of the congregation for these holidays attract so many people that they do not fit in the synagogue, and are held instead in a much larger, nearby church). The Next *Dor* High Holiday services attract a "standing room only" crowd of about 400 members of the 20s-30s age group.

Understanding the Constituency

While the activities of Next *Dor* DC have changed relatively little in the three years they have been operating, the program's success tends to build on itself, so that increasing numbers of participants join in. This is aided, no doubt, by the caliber of the participants, who (as Rabbi Zemel notes) are "not nerds: they're very serious, very questioning, very interested." In other words, they are the kind of people who attract peers to join them.

Although the gatherings have changed little in structure, the synagogue's understanding of the constituency has evolved considerably. Rabbi Lederman notes that the 20s-30s participants are really not a single constituency with shared characteristics; rather, she says, there are three sub-groups among which it is important to distinguish:

1. Young married people who have very young children (this is the constituency in which Rabbi Lederman situates herself). These people's core interests center on sorting out their lives, which have been radically shaken up by becoming parents; understanding the Jewish components of parenting; finding and building relationships with others in similar situations.

2. People in stable, committed couple relationships, whether married or not, gay or straight, who do not have children. These are generally people who have established or are establishing a relatively permanent home base in the DC area. Their career paths are becoming established. They have begun to develop settled roots, but may not yet have a network of relationships. They are looking for adult relationships with peers.

3. People who are not yet in stable, committed relationships. Often, they are at very early stages in their careers, and tend to change jobs frequently. In many senses, they are transients. They move often, and are involved in figuring out their own structures and patterns. Their interests are more social and their attention span is more short-term than those of the other groups.

Rabbi Lederman reports that it is difficult to create a group which caters to the needs of these three sub-populations at once.

Budget and Finances

The costs to Temple Micah for sponsoring the Next *Dor* DC project include half the salary of an Assistant Rabbi; $10,000 to $12,000 per year to hire a part-time outreach worker to support the Assistant Rabbi; $15,000 annually in expenses for Next *Dor* High Holy Day worship services; and about $2,500 annually in miscellaneous costs. Synagogue 3000 was initially contributing $40,000 annually towards these expenses. The organization's contribution is declining to zero over several years. Temple Micah has made the commitment to continue to fund the project fully as S3K support sunsets.

Underlying Philosophy

According to the Temple Micah website, the following principles undergird the Next *Dor* DC program:

1. *"Self-defined Jews* – We will not attempt to define who can be involved and who can't; all are welcome whether people self-identify as Jews or are in the process of self-identifying as a Jew or are connected to Jews in some way.
2. *"Team-driven vision* – Although much of the initial vision is being provided by Rabbi Lederman, our goal is to aim for a vision of this community that includes the voices of all who are stake-holders in this work.

3. *"Low-Bar to Engagement* – Our intention is to remove any obstacles to people becoming a part of this vibrant community; we will aim to make events metro-accessible, affordable, and walk-in friendly.

4. *"Experiment and take risks* – we really only learn what 'works' when we explore what hasn't been done, even it means making mistakes and learning along the way; this means any group of committed individuals who want to plan an event or try something new should begin making a plan!"

Factors and Key Dynamics Making for Success

Rabbis Zemel and Lederman attribute the success of Next *Dor* DC to its insistent pursuit of two key principles: (1) "Next *Dor* DC is a gateway, not a destination." The group is meant to serve participants as a gateway **to Jewish life**, not as a gateway to Temple Micah. (2) Next *Dor* DC is about relationships, not about events or programs. Its goal is to support and encourage its participants in developing a "thick" network of relationships. "Thick" in this context is meant to denote deep, multi-layered relationships which involve an implicit sense of responsibility and reciprocity.

Temple Micah has always adopted a slightly unconventional, forward-thinking, somewhat irreverent stance, which is doubtless attractive to many young people. A standing, self-deprecating in-joke among the Micah staff is: "I'm not in favor of organized religion either—I work at Temple Micah!"

The synagogue's lay leadership has always supported Next *Dor* DC as an expression of the synagogue's responsibility to invest in the next generation and in the larger Jewish community. It has taken the highly unusual stance of eschewing the temptation to force the program to serve the synagogue's institutional needs, and has resisted the temptation to make the program into a gateway to new membership in the synagogue. The sense that the synagogue is not "selling" something to participants is a key factor in keeping the group attractive.

Rabbi Zemel notes that success with this age cohort requires concentrated attention, and requires specialized skill sets. Rabbi Lederman is possessed of the requisite background and skills, and the synagogue has carved out an assignment for her which permits and expects that she devote the requisite concentrated attention.

What We Can Learn from Temple Micah and Next *Dor* DC

It is easy to see that Temple Micah is an unusual congregation. There are many ways in which the congregation is idiosyncratic, and it might therefore seem too much of an outlier to serve as a case study from which more typical congregations could learn.

For example, it is a congregation whose history and culture include an uncommon focus on youth and the contributions of members of the younger generation. Although nearly half a century has elapsed since the congregation's founding, the synagogue retains an unusual consciousness of, and appreciation for, the central role of young people in its establishment.

The synagogue has had the benefit of high-powered, charismatic rabbinic leadership for essentially all of its history. Additionally, there has been extraordinary stability of rabbinic leadership; the current senior rabbi has led the congregation for nearly three decades.

The congregation's location in Washington exposes it to congregants who represent an extraordinary pool of talent of the kind that is attracted to the District of Columbia, both for work within the government and its succession of administrations, and also for the vast array of not-for-profit agencies that are headquartered in the nation's capital.

Notwithstanding its above-noted idiosyncratic elements, there are many ways in which Temple Micah has built its Next *Dor* DC project that are wholly exemplary, in the sense that they serve as perfect exemplars of the principles which need to undergird programming for the 20s and 30s generation in order for it to be successful.

For one thing, Temple Micah demonstrates that a next generation project won't "just happen" spontaneously, but rather requires significant dedication of time, attention, resources and expertise. At Micah, these elements are provided by Rabbi Lederman, whose success would not be possible but for the fact that the synagogue has made it a priority. In other words, in order for the next generation project to succeed, there needs to be a decision at the highest level of congregational leadership to prioritize this work, and to dedicate the resources (of time, talent, energy and finances) required.

For a second thing, Temple Micah demonstrates that successful next generation outreach requires a specific skill-set of expertise and experience. Rabbi Lederman credits her background in community organizing for much of her approach to this work, and for its success. She says that a central principle of community organizing approach is never to do for a community of constituents what they are capable of doing for themselves. She notes that it is crucial to discern what next generation constituents can and cannot successfully do for themselves, as certain skills that are taken for granted in other (even only slightly older) generations are not necessarily widely available within this generation.

Third, Temple Micah demonstrates that a successful ministry to the 20s-30s generation must be a ministry that is about relationships, not about programs. People of this generation are over-programmed, and have too few opportunities to build genuine, satisfying, person-to-person, face-to-face relationships. Although this is a need they are generally not able to articulate, they respond to outreach that is grounded in genuine relationship-building. They are sensitive to hidden messages and resistant to sales pitches, so engagement must be genuine, and must not serve hidden agendas, such as growing the congregation's membership.

A fourth, corollary message is that in order to be successful in next generation engagement, the sponsoring congregation must undertake the project from motives related to the greater good of the community and of the individuals involved, and must eschew any intent for short-term, self-serving gain. In the case of Temple Micah, it is absolutely critical that both the synagogue's clergy and its board leadership have total clarity that short-term increase in the congregation's membership is not the goal of its next-generation outreach project. This is a particularly difficult message for many congregations, as it is natural for a board to take a position of resisting the expenditure of limited resources on projects unlikely to result in a visible return on investment, measured in the usual, fiscal terms. Challenging economic circumstances make this position much more difficult to resist.

Fifth, Temple Micah demonstrates that—in the Jewish community, at least—a project of engagement of 20s and 30s is most likely to succeed in an urban setting, where members of this generation are most likely to settle, at least temporarily. It is less clear how applicable this message is outside the Jewish community.

Sixth, the leadership of Temple Micah attributes the success of its Next *Dor* DC project at least in part to the casual informality of its worship space and style. As noted above, Temple Micah's worship is infused with humor and with music and with teaching. It is often interactive, and has a feeling-tone that often seems to echo what participants may have experienced (and appreciated) at summer camp.

Finally, the support of a central, national body (Synagogue 3000 in the case of Temple Micah's Next *Dor* DC program) has been immeasurably important in the success of the project. The central body has served many functions that have catalyzed the project at Temple Micah. (1) Identifying and naming the need to be filled: reaching out to engage the next generation in the life of the religious community. (2) Studying the extant literature on the topic, and identifying and articulating notable principles and practices; including, for example, the need for the work to be relationship-based rather than program-based; and the need to do the work for the sake of the greater good, not for short-term gain on the part of participating congregations. (3) Creating a community of practice which enables practitioners (in this case, Rabbi Lederman), to interact with and to learn from colleagues who are doing similar work—however differently—in other communities. (4) Generating a powerful incentive to initiate the work, in the form of financial grants to help underwrite the start-up costs of the project at the local level.

These seven elements—dedicated attention with adequate resources; outreach based in specialized skill-sets; a single-minded focus on relationship-building; commitment to doing the work for the sake of the greater good, not for short-term gain; the advantage of an urban setting; a style that is informal and which therefore projects a sense of being approachable; and the support of an outside body beyond the congregation—have proven to be critical in the success of Temple Micah's Next *Dor* DC project.

Although Temple Micah is an unusual, idiosyncratic congregation, its successful engagement program for the 20s-30s generation clearly demonstrates the importance of these seven critical elements, each of which is potentially replicable in virtually any congregational setting. Any congregation seeking to create a successful next generation outreach would do well to be informed by these elements in the experience of Temple Micah.

Rabbi Ramie Arian works as a consultant specializing in projects to engage young people in religious life. Much of his work involves project management and/or research relating to programs of experiential education, including, for example, summer camps and travel education.

References

Cohen, Steven M. and Hoffman, Lawrence A. (2011). *Different Growth for Different Folks: The ND Pilot Sites in Action.* Indianapolis: Synagogue 3000. (A formal study of four of the Next *Dor* pilot sites, including Temple Micah. This document is available upon request from Synagogue 3000 at 1075 Broad Ripple Avenue, Suite 216, Indianapolis, IN 46220 or by phone or email at (646) 783-1978 or info411@synagogue3000.org.)

Grossman, Cathy Lynn (2012). "Reverts Return to their Childhood Religions," *USA Today*, April 5, 2012. Available online at: http://www.usatoday.com/news/religion/story/2012-04-05/religion-catholic-baptist/54055072/1 (Includes a profile of Temple Micah and its role as part of Synagogue 3000's Next *Dor* initiative.)

Grossman, Ed (2011). "Next *Dor* Continues to Build on Early Success," *The Vine*, June-July-August 2011. A profile of the Next *Dor* group for Temple Micah's in-house newsletter, available online at: http://www.templemicah.org/newsfolder/newsitems/next-dor-continues-to-build-on-early-success/view

Lederman, Esther (n.d.). "I'm a Next *Dor* Rabbi." Published on line at: http://www.nextdoronline.org/profiles/blogs/im-a-next-dor-rabbi

Newsweek article listing Temple Micah as one of the 25 most dynamic Jewish congregations in the United States in 2009: http://www.thedailybeast.com/newsweek/2009/04/03/america-s-25-most-vibrant-congregations.html

National Next *Dor* initiative web site: www.nextdoronline.org.

Pollak, Suzanne (2011). "Singles Should be Included in Synagogue Life," *Washington Jewish Week*, December 21, 2011. Available online at: http://washingtonjewishweek.com/main.asp?Search=1&ArticleID=16333&SectionID=4&SubSectionID=4&S=1

Synagogue 3000 web site: www.synagogue3000.org.

Temple Micah web site: www.templemicah.org.

Chapter 12
The Well
Scotch Plains, New Jersey

By Gary S. Walter

The Well is a church-within-a-church ministry of Evangel Church, which is a member of the General Council of the Assemblies of God, the largest Pentecostal denomination in the world. They are located at 1251 Terril Road in Scotch Plains, New Jersey, a suburb of Newark and New York City. The ministry is pastored by Mandy Morante, whose husband, Chris Morante, at the time of this writing, was the interim senior pastor of the larger church body.

History and Overview

The Well began as a young adult ministry experiment in 2007. Pastor Chris Morante and his wife Mandy were fresh out of Bible College and had a vision and passion to serve God. They were given permission by senior Pastor Kevin Brennan to begin this ministry.

The Well meets for a weekly Sunday evening service, which is generally followed by a time of coffee and fellowship. Additionally, several times a year, there is a major Coffeehouse event designed primarily for fellowship. *The Well* also offers small groups and global mission opportunities.

Situated in a community that is surrounded by colleges and universities, *The Well* finds itself in constant attendance and population changes. The winter school terms always bring in fresh faces, but many of those students return to their homes during the summer. In addition, many students who attend college outside the area return to their home church after their time at school. Due to these challenges, there does not appear to be a significant growth trajectory; however, *The Well* continues with a stable attendance record.

Attendance averages 40 to 60 at the weekly service. Special services will sometimes draw as many as 80 or 90, and the quarterly Coffeehouse fellowship often draws about 120 people. When asked about the overall size of the congregation, Pastor Mandy suggested that they were reaching 200 to 250 people.

The larger church body of Evangel Church meets in two main services on Sunday morning, at 9 and 11 a.m. On a normal Sunday morning, between 1,600 and 1,800 attend, although there are only 900-plus members. From September to June, there is also a Sunday night service at 7 p.m., called the Encounter. This is a more contemporary-style service with extended worship and teaching. On Wednesday nights, a prayer service called Dwelling Place meets at 7 p.m. This consists of worship, a short teaching presentation, and prayer for various topics.

The community of *The Well* is made up primarily of young adults in their 20s, both single and married, and coming from various ethnic and racial backgrounds. There is a small percentage of people who are over 30 and, like other young adult ministries, *The Well* struggles to transition post-high school youth into their congregation. Services and programs are all in English.

Most of those participating in the ministry have been lifelong members of the sponsoring church and are connected with the Assemblies of God denomination. However, because *The Well* is the most successful young adult ministry in the area, people from other denominations and students who are not members are regular, if not frequent, attendees. Many of them consider *The Well* to be their home church and are not aware of the denominational connections; others are involved in other congregations in the region, but attend *The Well* for their own spiritual enrichment. Still others are hoping to give the Church one last chance before abandoning religion altogether.

Theology, Affiliation and Practices

Although the congregation is firmly Pentecostal in theology and practice, *The Well* does not focus too closely on this foundation. Where the larger church body may have more teaching in the gifts of the Spirit and the associated manifestations, the smaller young adult ministry rarely teaches about or expects these manifestations. The leadership team firmly believe in these and pray that they may one day occur, but because of the cross-denominational congregation, they are sensitive to differing beliefs. Like many young adult ministries throughout North America, the focus is more invitational and salvific, rather than doctrinal and prescriptive.

The leadership team is made up of the two founding pastors and eight other individuals who are very involved in various tasks and responsibilities. The majority of those serving in leadership at this writing were married couples in their late 20s, but recently they had been able to recruit some new leaders in their early 20s.

Evangel Church gave birth to *The Well* under Pastor Chris Morante's leadership. When Senior Pastor Kevin Brennan retired, Pastor Chris became the interim senior pastor and his wife, Pastor Mandy was assigned as the interim pastor of *The Well*. This unique situation allowed the leadership transitions to continue almost unnoticed and the congregation's fluid leadership team absorbed this change easily.

When *The Well* began as an experimental ministry, it was fully funded and approved by the mother church. Pastors Chris and Mandy were given a great amount of freedom to create and nurture the ministry. Early in the process, Senior Pastor Brennan offered confidence, strong mentoring, and permission to fail. It was this support that gave the young pastors what they needed to pursue their vision for the ministry.

Beginning in the fall of 2007, *The Well* sought to provide a strong worship service with great music, quality presentations, and strong preaching. The leadership team placed a premium on gifted musicians, solid technical skills, and enough financial resources to provide tools to that team. The audio, visual, and technical presentation are intended to produce what the team calls the "wow-factor." The stage is adorned artistically, with a black background, candles, good lighting, and musical instruments. There is a creative use of drama, video, and computer-generated graphics to accompany the presentations and sermons.

Various members of the leadership team are also regular preachers, and both men and women preach. The preaching team, like the congregation, is multi-ethnic and racially diverse. The worship leaders strive to bring in a healthy mix of pop culture while remaining solidly biblical, practical, and gospel-oriented.

Strengths

The Well is blessed with a strong and unified leadership team. The majority of the leaders have been together since the birth of this ministry, and it is clear they are modeling passion, vision, and service. They each share their gifts and strengths in ways that achieve success.

It is also clear that Pastors Mandy and her husband Chris are strong leaders and their vision is the driving force in *The Well*. This is not to say that others do not share that passion, or are overshadowed by this pastoral team; only that their leadership is what brings focus and direction to the ministry.

Two solid best practices within this young adult congregation include the preaching and worship experiences. The leadership includes several very capable speakers who are able to rotate into this role. Many successful young adult ministries make use of multiple preachers and speakers. *The Well* seems to have found this to be true.

There are several accomplished musicians that enable the weekly worship experience to be one of quality and substance. This undoubtedly is a very positive strength and enables them to attract young adults from around the region.

Technology is a major strength also. From the website to the weekly worship experience, *The Well* obviously has some gifted technologists working for them. Each service is broadcast live and posted on the web for later viewing. The production quality online and live is very good.

Not only has *The Well* survived for five years at this time, but it has maintained a solid focus and continues to reach new people. Their ministry functions are well thought out and well attended. The church is ministering internally and externally, locally, nationally, and globally.

Locally: In addition to a solid weekly worship experience that reaches young adults in real and relevant ways, they have a campus ministry to deliver care packages to students from out of town. This cross-denominational outreach helps students find a faith community when they are away from their hometown churches.

One of the more successful ministries of *The Well* is their occasional coffeehouse fellowship. This is primarily a social event that draws students and young adults from various backgrounds and denominations. It usually draws more people than the other activities, but is also a more transient population. Although *The Well* also advertises small groups, this does not appear to be as strong a ministry as the coffeehouse.

Nationally: In the Fall of 2010, *The Well* sponsored a young adult Thirst Conference that attracted over 500 participants, primarily from the tri-state, New York, New Jersey, and Pennsylvania area. Another event was planned as of this writing, but put on hold during the leadership transitions.

Globally: Over the past five years, the church has gone to Africa three times and sponsored the digging of five wells in various communities which previously were without water. They have also built two steel structures and added brick to one of the buildings. One is used as an HIV Care Center and Orphanage and the other as a church.

Weaknesses

As mentioned earlier, due to the transient nature of student populations, *The Well* struggles to keep young adults that walk in the doors. Not only are many of these students only in the area for nine months or less during the year, but many do not return to the same school. The time challenges faced by students also makes it difficult for them to commit.

Some students attend once a month, or less, many are not affiliated with the Assemblies of God denomination, and still others attend for mostly social interests. This not only makes it difficult to attract people who are willing to serve, but also limits opportunities to attract and mentor new leaders. These issues are common to young adult ministries, especially in college towns.

The leadership team of *The Well* is a cohesive group of young adults, but as they grow older, they will find themselves older than the target age of the young adults they seek to attract. This too is a common problem of young adult ministries. The success of the team begins to be a weakness in attracting younger members and leaders.

In addition, the more active leaders are married couples and within young adult ministries there can be a sharp demarcation between married and single congregants.

Currently, not many high school students and youth are successfully making the transition to the young adult ministry. This too is a common issue. At 18/19 years old, recent high school graduates no longer feel the draw to youth ministries that include much younger teen students. However, the ability to integrate themselves into a more mature group of young adults is an intimidating prospect.

Older teen girls may feel like prey, and older teen boys, who tend to mature more slowly than their female peers, may feel lost in the social sea of young adults. It takes intentional efforts to integrate the graduating youth into a young adult ministry. However, a ministry that struggles to find new leaders and solid members, is often focused on maintaining the ministry for the core and will often not have the resources to reach into its fringes, which would include the incoming youth.

Recently a younger member joined the leadership team and that has encouraged the rest of the team. However, some of the leadership and members are now in their 30s. This will necessitate some leadership introspection about the future of The Well.

Vision

From the beginning, Pastors Chris and Mandy possessed a love and compassion for young adults. Their hearts longed to reach their peers with a real and relevant gospel message. Not only did they desire to be good role models and mentors, but they sought the same for themselves. They found this in Pastor Brennan and Evangel Church.

The larger church offered solid support for the idea and birth of The Well. They were given permission to be creative. They were given financial resources and the facility to build and grow this ministry. They were provided solid prayer support, trust, and experienced coaching as The Well developed its foundation and footing. Importantly, this experiment and its young leaders were given permission to fail.

From its earliest days, the leadership team operated with full cooperation and support from the larger church body. This is a common thread in successful young adult ministries. Support from the church and denomination is integral to the birth and maturation of the ministry.

Early in the development of *The Well* came the vision of satiating thirst - not just spiritual, but physical thirst. This idea inspires the worship experiences and the mission outreach— as witness wells for Africa and college care packages to meet physical as well as emotional needs of displaced college students. This compassion is a driving force in the pastoral team and lived out through the leadership and servants within the congregation.

Changes

Over time *The Well*, like many ministries, has sought balance between substance and image. Knowing that churches are often evaluated based on numbers, and knowing that sufficient numbers of people bring with them the financial resources to sustain and grow the church, it was important to provide a significantly attractive worship experience and program.

On the other hand, it is the substance of the Gospel that provides the health and vitality of all churches. While most older, traditional church models focus on substance and stability, young adult congregations don't have this luxury. Young adults, especially those looking to leave the outmoded services of their childhood churches, are looking for a congregation that more closely reflects their tastes and culture.

Church leaders who seek to provide both solid biblical substance, along with new methods, face a challenge of balance with few patterns to follow. *The Well* has sometimes focused on the substance of the Gospel message, and at other times catered to the style and appearance that would draw people into the services and programs of the church.

Currently, the leadership team is moving towards more substance—with less concern about attendance numbers. While they understand this is the right approach, there is some hesitation to alienate their already fickle attendees. They understand that some young adults have a history of disillusionment with the Church. *The Well* may be a last chance for some to connect with a faith community and the leadership team understand they have to be careful.

Pastor Mandy paraphrased a text from Jeremiah that represented the leader's conviction. They know their approval must come from God, and not from the people. This is challenging when a group feels called to be culturally relevant. To meet people where they are, without compromising the message, is usually the driving purpose of most contemporary pastors.

To bring the gospel to the alienated, wounded, and broken people, in ways that speak to them and draw them to Christ, is the whole reason pastors have left traditional ministries. They see people who have lost hope in the traditional Church, but are still looking for God and a culturally relevant faith community. At the same time, pastors are loyal to their Church roots and are not anxious to leave all of that behind.

Those who do not bridge this gap successfully and find the balance point between substance and relevance will find themselves with either a dying ministry or unemployed. As of this writing, *The Well* and its leadership has successfully navigated this path. As they go through leadership transitions, it will be interesting to watch them in the future.

The leadership team knows their future success is not reliant on the lights, the music, and the cafe. From this point forward they will emphasize the substance of their preaching and teaching, without diminishing the technical quality of the service.

Challenges

The biggest challenge facing the ministry is in the transient nature of their target audience. The population changes depending on the weather school is in session or on Summer break. It is also affected by the major vacation breaks that occur mid-semester in fall, winter, and spring.

Indeed, young adults and students are very non-committal and reluctant to attend institutionalized events and programs. The advent of the mobile web has only aggravated this issue. While some will still choose to congregate, web applications like Foursquare, Twitter, and Facebook has made it easier to assess, in real time, where their peers are gathering. Leaders are then left to plan activities which people may or may not choose to attend.

This is also a challenge facing the recruitment of volunteers and those needed for the successful administration of ministry projects. While a small percentage is faithful in attendance and participation, a larger percentage is much more fickle and harder to recruit. Solid commitments are rare in the younger generations. This is a challenge that all churches will soon face, but is primarily a young adult issue currently.

As mentioned earlier, due to the lower attendance numbers, *The Well* is not fully self-funded. They rely on financial and facility support from the larger church. While this is an import ministry of Evangel Church, in order for *The Well* to truly thrive, they will need to become more self-sufficient and seek greater growth and maturity.

Also mentioned earlier is the aging of the leadership team. Most church growth experts recognize that leaders attract people within 10 years of their own age. While this is not a hard and fast rule, it generally holds true. As the pastoral team enters their 30s, they will begin to attract older adults, also in their thirties and even older. Their ability to attract the 18-20 year old graduating youth will be hampered by this same progression of age.

Many successful young adult ministries from the 1990s have ceased to be young adult congregations. The ministry itself has graduated in a full-fledged church that caters to younger suburban families - complete with children's programs and senior activities. *The Well* is rapidly approaching a time when this will be a real issue. Most ministries do not tackle this with intentionality, but tend to drift into these changes without much forethought.

Opportunities

Like many leaders of churches that want to be real and relevant, the leadership team at *The Well* does not want to measure their success in numbers or data. Instead they want their success to be assessed through the changed lives of people. Typically this is more difficult. Financial data, attendance records, and baptisms are easy to measure. Currently there is not a good measurement matrix for "changed lives."

Optimistically, the leadership of *The Well* is looking to their obedience to God's direction and leaving the success, or failure, in His hands. This is a tremendous opportunity, but few ministry teams have successfully navigated this path. Generally, what gets measured is where growth happens. This is the opportunity that faces not just *The Well* and Evangel Church, but all relevant ministries of the future. As we develop a matrix and significant benchmarks to measure discipleship, life change, and changed lives, we, as a Church, can better serve our people in more significant ways.

Lessons Learned

For congregation that wish to support a young adult ministry, or church planters who choose to focus on the young adult population, there are several lessons to be learned:

1. *Leadership is crucial.* Selecting leaders of character, integrity, calling, and purpose is essential. Leaders must have passion, compassion, and vision. Leaders must be persons of prayer with a solid biblical foundation. Leaders must be gifted and experienced in leading—in other words, they must be able to attract followers, collaborators, and teammates.

2. *Church support is essential.* Without the support of the denomination, overseers, ministry organization, or mother church, the ministry will not succeed. This support must be organic and not coerced. From the senior pastor/leader, through the board, and deep into the congregation/stakeholders, the support must be spiritual, philosophical, missional, and financial.

3. *Worship must be experiential and experimental.* As witnessed at *The Well*, the worship experience, as well as the coffee house ministry, is an experience that draws young adults looking for something real and relevant. Quality is important, but it must support the experience, not overshadow it. Indeed, the leadership needs permission to experiment, change, adapt, and enhance the whole of the ministry, as well as individual pieces.

4. *Vision and purpose must be clear and be clearly stated.* Many young adult and contemporary ministries begin out of rebellion and this is difficult DNA to outgrow. The ministry must be birthed from a vision and purpose to do something significant. Pastors Chris and Mandy have demonstrated this passion from an early age and it shows in the success and longevity of *The Well*.

5. *Outreach and service outside the church body must be included.* *The Well* has demonstrated local and global mission in ways that few small congregations do. Not only have they reached inward to build the local ministry, but they have reached outward to local college students and global mission projects. This enables the congregants to avoid a selfishness that often stifles personal and community growth.

6. Love wins. One thing that resonates strongly from the leadership of *The Well* is their love for others, love for God, and love for each other. This essential principle, lived out in a community of faith, is a powerful glue. It not only binds the leaders together, but attracts others who come within reach.

Conclusion

While most church leaders would like to downplay the place of personality when it comes to ministry success, it is difficult to ignore. When spirituality, personality, giftedness, and vision come together with the right mix, the ministry will often flourish. When the ministry does not succeed, it is often easy to see how these qualities were not well mixed.

Sometimes a single individual will rise up and lead a successful ministry to unforeseen successes. Often it will be a team of individuals who cooperate with unique talents and gifts to birth a successful ministry. Other times, the leadership is so organic, that it is difficult to really ascertain the source of vision and the real work in its success.

When it comes to *The Well*, it is apparent, even from a distance, that Senior Pastor Kevin Brennan is a big part of the success of this young adult ministry. His vision, support, and enthusiasm are frequently mentioned by the current leader of the ministry. But that is not to in any way diminish the calling and giftedness of the Morantes. It is clear that their love for their peers is a significant component of *The Well*.

It is important to further research young adult ministries, the changing demographics of generational ministry, and the role played by more mature adult congregations. Style has to be real and relevant to the target population, but other than that, it isn't style that determines success. The granular mosaic of people, spiritual gifts, and teamwork are where we do not possess sufficient benchmarks for growth, success, discipleship, and mission. Without a better understanding of less tangible data, it will be difficult for church leaders to replicate successes like *The Well*.

The difficulty of providing a ministry to a target generation, like young adults, is that people continue to age and mature. Early on the creators of the ministry must decide if they are going to remain relevant to a certain age group, or if they will evolve and mature with their initial target group.

To use the business world as a model, there are stores which attempt to provide all things to all people, so-called "big box" stores, and others which cater to only one cohort, such as a store selling children's toys, or one selling clothing to "big and tall men." Full-service, traditional congregations, would like to be all things to all people. However, there may be groups within their congregations, such as youth and young adults, who feel they are often left with the leftovers. This leaves them unsatisfied and disillusioned. So young adult ministries start up, but they usually don't imagine staying with their first attendees and becoming a full-service church.

Because of the normal path transition from young adult ministry to full-service church, most young adult ministries that showed great success in the 1990s no longer exist as young adult congregations. It would be interesting to study those that made a successful transition and how that was accomplished.

It would also be fascinating to develop a survey of existing young adult congregations, whether they exist as a ministry, a church within a church, or as a stand-alone community of faith. Crucial to the survey would be to find common denominators, outliers, and common traits.

Some questions that should be included in a survey include: (1) Are the successful young adult congregations affiliated with a denomination or national parachurch ministry organization? (2) Does the ministry have a growth plan? (3) Has the community developed a strategy to remain focused on young adults, or do they have a plan to mature into a church for young families? (4) What is the purpose and focus of the ministry? Is it spirituality, discipleship, worship, meeting social needs, mission-oriented, service-oriented or did it begin as a rebellion? (5) Were there significant phases within their history that provided opportunities or challenges that are common across the nation? This could be a measure of time, attendance, measurement, or programs—or all of the above.

Many would like to see holistic congregations that minister to all ages, all worship styles, all socioeconomic groups, and all races and ethnicities, but this is rarely possible. The fallback is that we cater to each of these groups individually. It is important to overcome the silos of isolation, impediments to outreach and service, and the financial obstacles. Indeed, even political and preferential issues can overshadow the needs of forgotten people groups, like young adults.

Further research into successes and failures will help church leaders know what is profitable to pursue, and what is not. Without significant data, all decisions are made based on preference and prejudice - both good and bad in their own ways.

One new trend that is rising in popularity is city-wide, ecumenical young adult gatherings. These gatherings are not full-service ministries, but they do provide the opportunity for quality generationally-targeted worship experiences that meet the needs and expectations of the target audience.

Whatever the path, there should be enough outcome-based data to determine what enables a young adult ministry to succeed or fail. The challenge will be to track down that data and talk to the people who were involved.

Gary S. Walter left a rewarding and respected emergency services career in 1995 to complete a B.A. in business at La Sierra University. Surprisingly, he found himself involved at Young & Restless Ministries, a very successful and dynamic young adult church within a church that regularly attracted 500 attendees. After seminary at Andrews University, Gary and his wife Jennifer planted an experimental, cell-based church community in Colorado Springs. Currently Gary is a freelance pastor and writer living in Portland, Oregon.

References

Barna, George (n.d.). "Six Reasons Young Christians Leave Church." http://www.barna.org/teens-next-gen-articles/528-six-reasons-young-christians-leave-church

Charlotte One: http://charlotteone.org/

Evangel Church web site: www.evangelchurch.com/

Generations defined: en.wikipedia.org/wiki/List_of_generations#List_of_generations

"Pastors Call a Truce on 'Sheep-Stealing," *Wall Street Journal*. http://online.wsj.com/article/SB10001424052702304743704577380423751492552.html

The Well, Evangel Church, 1251 Terril Road, Scotch Plains, New Jersey 07076; (908) 322-9300.

The Well web site: http://thewellnj.com/

Thirst Conference: www.facebook.com/thirstconference

"Young Adults are Abandoning Church in Record Numbers: Is This the Solution?" http://www.theblaze.com/stories/young-adults-are-abandoning-churches-in-record-numbers-is-this-the-solution/

Chapter 13
Best Practices for Congregations

By Perry Chang

Starbucks? Yes. Boring worship? No.

Involving people from their late teens to early 30s in congregational leadership, having high-quality and innovative worship, and accepting people with their coffee cups, shorts, and diverse theologies are all critical parts of incorporating younger people into congregations. Having young adult-only or young adult-heavy worshiping communities, nested inside of existing congregations or as stand-alone congregations, can also be important. Even starting new intergenerational worshiping communities or moving existing congregations to new locations can help.

These are findings of a landmark Cooperative Congregational Studies Partnership (CCSP)/Faith Communities Today (FACT) young adult incorporation study. The study included: (1) a sweeping review of existing studies about young-adult involvement in congregations; (2) a penetrating analysis of 2010 FACT survey data; and (3) a dozen or so innovative case studies of congregations from various faith traditions with heavy young-adult involvement. The partnership brings together religious researchers and religious leaders from more than 40 U.S. Christian denominations and other faith groups who provide research-based resources to promote congregational vitality.

Participation in U.S. religious communities has been declining for decades, but attendance by young adults has decreased more rapidly, notes Princeton researcher LiErin Probasco in her literature review. As adolescence extends into "emerging adulthood," young people have been marrying later and having children later. At the same time, fewer and fewer single or childless people have been involved in congregations. These trends account for a share of young adults' disappearance from the pews, Probasco maintains. Young adults' increasing anti-institutionalism and lack of theological orthodoxy and the fact that the fraction of the U.S. population in this age group has been shrinking have also contributed.

In spite of these developments, some U.S. congregations have been successful at incorporating young adults, note Probasco and CCSP/FACT researchers Monte Sahlin and David Roozen. Sahlin and Roozen analyzed findings of the 2010 FACT survey, the fourth in a series of surveys that have typically mixed surveys of congregations within FACT member faith communities with surveys of random samples of U.S. congregations. The two researchers focused on congregations in which more than one in five participants (21 percent or more) are between 18 and 34 years old. One in six (16 percent) of the 11,000 congregations surveyed fall in this category.

Many of the three researchers' findings confirm what the case-study researchers found. The case-study researchers mixed interviewing, observation, and archival and web research.

In Leadership

Intentionally involving young adults in leadership is something many of the case-study worshiping communities do. This is, of course, the case for young adult-only congregations and young adult worshiping communities within congregations. For example, at the Harriman (Utah) Latter Day Saints (LDS or "Mormon") all-young single adult congregation, outside of Salt Lake City, most members receive a "calling." A pastoral leader asks the member to serve on 1 of the congregation's 12 committees. The committees arrange most of the congregation's activities, and one of the committees sends its members out to visit members of the congregation who have not participated recently. In addition, about one-third of members visit other members each month to share an evangelical message.

Intergenerational congregations with large young adult attendance, however, also have young adults in leadership. At the Baha'i Center of Houston, for example, 1 in 10 congregational board members are young adults, and most teachers of classes for children and youth and half of the rotating worship leaders are young adults. The Baha'i' faith originated in Iran in the 1800s and draws from most world religions.

Having younger people in long-term pastoral and worship leadership also seems important. In 3 of the 10 worshiping communities studied, pastoral or worship leaders are in their 20s or early 30s. In 3 more, pastoral leaders are in their 40s.

Both of the case-study congregational leaders in their 20s are women. Krista Kutz is a liturgical minister at Old St. Patrick's Roman Catholic Church in Chicago, and Mandy Morante is the pastor of The Well, a young adult-only worshiping community that is part of Evangel Church, an Assembly of God-affiliated congregation in suburban New Jersey.

Quality Worship Experience

The seven researchers who attended worship at the case-study communities they studied all commented on the worship's high quality, and all but one also described the worship as informal, innovative, or experimental. Young adult attendees interviewed also commented on this as something that has attracted and kept them in the communities.

Many of the large case-study congregations use state-of-the-art video and projection technology and top-notch musicians and vocalists on their worship teams. For example, at ChristWay Community Church, a Southern Baptist-affiliated congregation outside of Chattanooga (Tennessee), musicians who are part of the worship team must audition. At Sunday worship services at Chicago's New Life Covenant Church, performances by the congregation's 15-member dance team and videos with announcements presented in the form of news reports are projected on the huge screens in the University of Illinois at Chicago's cavernous auditorium, where the congregation currently worships.

Half of the 10 case-study worshiping communities include guitars and drums in their worship services. On the one hand, even a small, mainline Protestant congregation— Atlanta's Kirkwood United Church of Christ—uses guitars and projection equipment. On the other hand, with half of the case-study worshiping communities attracting sizable numbers of young adults without these markers of "contemporary" worship style, contemporary worship is apparently not an absolute requirement for young adult participation.

This is consistent with the FACT 2010 results, which showed that roughly half of young adult-heavy congregations use electric guitar and bass regularly. These instruments are used by twice as many of these young adult-heavy congregations as they are by other congregations.

Catholic and Orthodox case-study congregations, in particular, have more traditional worship, but young adults still find the worship appealing. Commented a young adult attending worship at Chicago's Old St. Patrick's Roman Catholic Church for the first time: "I recognize all the hymns from the Catholic Church I grew up in but I have never
heard them performed so beautifully." He said the music was both "familiar" and "fresh."

Innovation

Innovation and use of technology by young adult-heavy congregations extend beyond worship to communication. Half a dozen of the case-study congregations use Facebook or Twitter to communicate with people involved in their worshiping communities. At Spokane's Life Center, young adult-heavy small groups share prayer requests via text message, and at the Boston area's St. Mary Orthodox Church

252

the priest texts daily inspirational messages to parishioners. At Tennessee's ChristWay Community, the pastor invites worshipers to follow along with the scripture passages and his sermon notes via applications on their Smartphone's. All of this is consistent with findings from Sahlin and Roozen's analysis of FACT 2010 survey results. FACT 2010 congregations with significant use of technology were twice as likely to be young adult-heavy as were congregations with minimal use of technology.

For the case-study congregations, innovation led congregations in other directions too. Half of the case-study congregations have developed events popular with young adults that cross the line between worship and secular social events. Some of these events take place outside of conventional congregational spaces. Kirkwood, Old St. Pat's, and Temple Micah sponsor events that mix drinking and theological reflection: Kirkwood's "Wine Down Wednesdays," Micah's "Drinks and Drash," and Old St. Pat's "Theology on Tap." Drinks and Drash takes place each time in a different restaurant or bar near where young adult worshipers work. The LDS's Herriman congregation has a dry "Mix and Mingle" night and a talent show, and a number of members play with each other on local volleyball teams. Spokane's Life Center, affiliated with the International Church of the Foursquare Gospel, sponsors half a dozen College Houses, where students linked with the congregation live, pray, and serve together. Another example is Old St. Pat's "World's Largest Block Party." Planning, executing, and recovering from this epic event absorb so much of the time and energy of the congregation's staff and other leaders that it was not easy for the researcher studying Old St. Pat's to complete her research in June, when the block party takes place.

Hospitality

At 7 of the 10 case-study congregations, researchers or young-adult participants describe the congregations as very "accepting," both of young adults and of people in general. At 3 of the 10 congregations, that means giving worshipers the option of not "dressing up" for worship. At 6 of the 10 congregations, that means providing food and coffee or permitting worshipers to bring coffee into worship. Offering pizza, nachos, breakfast food, barbeque, and even espresso seems to help nurture and keep young adults in the fold. At Tennessee's ChristWay, biennial outdoor baptism celebrations out in the pond in front of congregational facilities feature hot dogs, lawn chairs, and cheering crowds. At ChristWay's indoor services, worshipers are encouraged to bring their free coffee (provided by the congregation) into worship. Researcher Carole Kilcher's observation about ChristWay was repeated by other researchers and their informants about the other worshiping communities too: "The philosophy that this is a place to 'come as you are' with no need to dress up gives young adults a place with a Starbucks-like feel where they know they will be accepted and find a place to belong."

"Don't judge" is a mantra repeated at Spokane's Life Center, signaling that "accepting" also means tolerating theological diversity. At The Well, which is designed to be interdenominational and draws some young adults from other area congregations, this means de-emphasizing The Well's parent church's teachings about speaking in tongues. At Kirkwood, this means welcoming homosexual Christians, Republicans, and "even people who support Chick-Fil-A because that's the gospel of Jesus."

At Old St. Patrick's, being accepting also means permitting young adults (whose lives, schedules, and locales change frequently) to serve on committees without having to make multi-year committee service commitments. And at Temple Micah, being accepting means waiving the fees for participation in young adult-only High Holidays worship services.

Reaching Out

At the case-study congregations, having a large number of young adults is not something that has happened by accident. Congregational leaders have been intentional about connecting with people age 18 to 34. Leaders of half of FACT young adult-heavy congregations also indicated that their congregations have a "strong" emphasis on young adult ministry.

Also, in 7 of the 10 case-study congregations, the pastoral leaders have made incorporating young adults a personal priority. At Atlanta's Kirkwood and D.C.'s Temple Micah, the pastors helped start young adult fellowships by inviting young adults over to their homes. At St. Mary's Orthodox Church in Cambridge (Massachusetts), recent priests have served as Orthodox chaplains at the neighboring Harvard University and Massachusetts Institute of Technology, and one of the priests has been active at New England camps where many area Orthodox youth spend time before they become young adults.

Emphasizing young adult outreach should not make congregational leaders seem like used car salesmen, caution researchers and informants in three case studies. Young adults are looking for "authentic" experiences and looking like one is trying to "sell" something is a sure way to seem inauthentic, they warn. For example, Kirkwood's seminary intern describes the congregation in this way: "I think we are really authentic. We are not doing this in a smarmy way, but we really are because we live it. What you see is what you get. (The pastor) has been firm with me that we don't want to be a 'slick church,' so we've found a beautiful balance between doing something nice with care and still being authentic."

Investing in Young People

Similarly, if an existing, intergenerational congregation is trying to incorporate more young adults into its ranks or into a special worshiping community nested within it, they will likely need to invest time, energy, and money into this initiative without expecting this necessarily to land them more members or to pay for itself in giving by new young adult attendees.

"It is absolutely critical that the (congregation's) leadership have total clarity that short- term increase in the congregation's membership is not the goal of its next-generation outreach project," writes Temple Micah researcher Ramie Arian. "This is a particularly difficult message for many congregations, as it is natural to take a position of resisting the expenditure of limited resources on projects unlikely to result in a visible return on investment, measured in the usual, fiscal terms."

Two case-study congregations have received denominational or parachurch support for young adult initiatives. It seems likely that the Herriman congregation is subsidized by the LDS denomination, whose finances are centralized, and Temple Micah was given financial support by a cross-denominational Jewish organization. All 10 of the case- study worshiping communities are linked with denominations, but only half of them emphasize this link.

Young adult worshiping communities associated with two larger congregations—Temple Micah's Next DOR DC and Evangel Church's The Well—are being subsidized by their parent congregations, also.

Newcomers

Young adult-heavy FACT 2010 congregations have been founded disproportionately more recently, and case-study congregations have followed suit. About two-thirds (7 out of 10) of the case-study worshiping communities were either founded since 1999 or moved to their current location since 1999. The newest is Herriman's LDS congregation, which was re-organized as a young single adult-only congregation in

2011. Chicago's New Life Covenant Church is planning to move worship locations shortly.

One exception is Chicago's Old St. Patrick's, which was founded in 1846. Old St. Patrick's reputation as a beautiful, old, historic, Irish-American church and church home of former Mayor Richard M. Daley has helped make this congregation a popular wedding locale for metro Chicago area young adults The congregation's marriage preparation activities (mandatory for aspiring St. Pat's newlyweds), in turn, funnel engaged couples into its late Sunday afternoon mass, which is popular with young adults.

Location, Location, Location

One factor that appears in both the FACT 2010 data and the case-study findings is largely outside of congregational control. The FACT 2010 young adult-heavy congregations are disproportionately found in urban and suburban areas, as well as

high-population growth areas. Case-study congregations are located in a litany of large metropolitan areas: Atlanta, Boston, Chicago, Houston, and Washington (D.C.), for example. Some are also located in areas with a large concentration of college students. In Chicago, New Life Covenant Church actually worships on the campus of the University of Illinois at Chicago. In Atlanta, Kirkwood United Church of Christ draws energy and leadership from half a dozen students at Atlanta area seminaries.

Whether your congregation or prospective new congregational development site is located in a big city or small town or in a college town or a 55-plus community, whether you're a 50-something organizing pastor or a 20-something layperson in an existing congregation wanting to worship with more young adults; is it worth the trouble to try to connect with people in their late teens to early 30s?

Yes, say case-study researchers and informants resoundingly. Says Bridger, a Herriman worshiper, about the concentration of young adults in that congregation: "We're in it together. We're in the same situation, and it's fun." Adds one of Bridger's peers at Herriman: "I'm celebrating my one-year anniversary of coming back to the church after spending a while on some undesirable paths. I am grateful for my second chance with the church."

Armed with important insight and information, perhaps actual and potential U.S. congregations too will have a "second chance" to incorporate more young adults into their congregations.

Perry Chang teaches sociology at Bellarmine University and Jefferson Community and Technical College in Louisville, Kentucky. For eight years Chang conducted survey and focus group research for the Presbyterian Church (U.S.A.). His research dealt with issues such as congregational growth and the development of multicultural congregations. He also advised congregations involved in mission discernment. Chang served as program chair for the 2013 annual meeting of the Religious Research Association in Boston. He also served as chair of the membership committee for the Cooperative Congregational Studies Partnership. Chang has served as a ruling elder at Crescent Hill Presbyterian Church.

Appendix
The Faith Communities Today Surveys

Faith Communities Today (FACT) is the series title for national interfaith studies of local religious congregations conducted collaboratively by the major faiths in America through the Cooperative Congregational Studies Partnership (CCSP). Major surveys were conducted in 2000, 2005, 2008 and 2010. Future surveys of similar reach and sample size will be implemented in 2015, 2020 and beyond.

The FACT 2010 data set (on which the first chapter of this volume is based as well as references elsewhere) brought together 26 individual surveys which are listed below. A total of 24 of these were conducted by or for denominations and faith groups representing 32 of the nation's largest religious traditions.

American Baptist Churches USA
Assemblies of God
Baha'i of the United States
Christian Church (Disciples of Christ)
Christian Reformed Church
Church of Jesus Christ of Latter-day Saints
Church of the Nazarene
Churches of Christ
Conservative Judaism (Synagogue 3000)
Episcopal Church
Evangelical Lutheran Church in America
Historically Black Denominations (Interdenominational Theological Center)
Lutheran Church Missouri Synod
Mennonite Church USA
Muslim (Islamic Society of America)
Non-denominational Congregations (Hartford Institute for Religion Research)
Orthodox Christian (Standing Conference of Canonical Orthodox Bishops in America)
Presbyterian Church (U.S.A.)

Reformed Church in America
Reform Judaism (Synagogue 3000)
Roman Catholic Church (Center for Applied Research in the Apostolate)
Seventh-day Adventist Church
Southern Baptist Convention
Unitarian Universalist Association
United Church of Christ
United Methodist Church
Non-partner traditions surveyed by a subcontractor of CCSP

The partners developed a common core questionnaire of just over 150 items, including items from the previous surveys. Copies of all the instruments are available at the Web site www.faithcommunitiestoday.org/.

Using the common questionnaire, CCSP partner groups conducted their own, typically mail and online surveys of a representative, random national sample of their own congregations. Usually a congregation's leader completed the questionnaire. CCSP also conducted a national survey of non-denominational congregations based on a random sample drawn from several mailing and marketing lists purchased from vendors. Finally, CCSP contracted with a denominational agency to survey a sample of congregations from non-partner faiths, also based on a random sample drawn from several mailing and marketing lists.

For purposes of the overall national analysis, the 26 FACT 2010 sub-surveys were combined in such a way that, through the use of statistical weights, each partner denomination and faith group, and each non-partner cluster of congregations are represented in the national data set proportionate to their representation in the total population of congregations in the United States. This aggregated data set includes responses from 11,077 congregations, and over 120 denominations/faiths.

Response rates were typically good for surveys of this type; in the 40 percent range. Sampling error for a survey such as FACT 2010 can only be roughly estimated. We believe a conservative estimate is plus or minus four percentage points at the 95 percent confidence level.

Questions, comments and requests to be added to the FACT Newsletter email list should be sent to Monte Sahlin at msahlin@creativeministry.org. The newsletter will announce future FACT surveys and research reports.

Made in the USA
Columbia, SC
24 March 2022

58105258R00143